Season of Glad Songs
A Christmas Anthology

Season of Glad Songs

A Christmas Anthology
Tessa Bielecki and David Denny

Sand & Sky Publishing

Sand and Sky Publishing is an imprint of the Desert Foundation, an informal circle of friends exploring the wisdom of the world's deserts with a special focus on peace and reconciliation between the three Abrahamic traditions that grow out of the desert: Judaism, Christianity, and Islam. Proceeds from the sale of this book support the Desert Foundation, a 501 (c)(3) organization founded in June 2005 by Tessa Bielecki and David Denny. Contributions are tax-deductible.

Sand and Sky Publishing
P.O. Box 1000
Crestone, CO 81131

www.desertfound.org
sandandsky@desertfound.org
Available at www.CreateSpace.com/4184188

Book design and composition by Tessa Bielecki
Cover design and computer graphics by David Denny
Cover artwork © Fotosearch.com

Manufactured in the United States of America
ISBN-13: 978-0615918143 (Sand and Sky Publishing)
ISBN-10: 061591814X

For those
who keep Christmas in their hearts
all year long

Contents

Part 1: Advent

Part 2: Winter

Part 3: Christmas

Poetry

Rituals, Prayers and Blessings

Music, Movie and Reading Reflections

Part 4: The New Year

Poetry

Rituals, Prayers and Blessings

Music, Movie and Reading Reflections

Part 5: Epiphany

Rituals, Prayers and Blessings

Part 6: Candlemas

Acknowledgements

We are grateful to Laura Keim, Dennis Brown, Paul Baynham, Pegge Erkeneff, Kristen Kauffman, and Netanel Miles-Yepez, who encourage our vocations as contemplatives and writers. They also support us by serving on the Desert Foundation Board of Directors.

Netanel first urged us to "harvest" our writings from the past forty years and suggested we create Sand and Sky Publishing.

We are also grateful to those who subscribe to our newsletter, *Caravans*, and visit the Desert Foundation web site, especially Ruth Hoffman and Dorie Friend.

We couldn't have created this book without "Miss X," who scanned many of these chapters and did the original editing. Then she became an avid and competent proofreader. And in between, she helped us prune trees around our hermitages and cut firewood for the winter.

From 1970–2004, when we were Carmelite monks in the Spiritual Life Institute, one or the other or both of us edited the community's magazine, *Desert Call*. During those years, Terry Sullivan (now Prevéy) and Leslie McNamara became two of our artists and dear friends. Deborah Dyer came into our lives later, often sending us illustrated letters. We are glad to share the artistry of these women now with a larger circle of readers. Some of the writing included here was originally published in *Desert Call* and appears now in revised form.

Can Stock Photo Inc., located in Halifax, Nova Scotia, is a group of talented artists who delighted us with their wide variety of illustrations. When we got tired of words, we looked at their art for the sheer joy of it.

CreateSpace is also a remarkable company, producing software that makes self-publishing easier than we ever imagined. Whenever we needed help from a human being instead of a computer program, someone always called us back and responded personally, generously and clearly—within five minutes every time.

We are enormously grateful to Joanne and Gary Boyce and the Nicholas and Pansy Schenck Foundation. When we were homeless, they built hermitages for us adjacent to their cattle ranch, silent and solitary spaces where we write, pray, and live out our lives as contemplatives and writers.

Lastly, we are grateful to our parents, our grandparents, and our extended families, from whom we first learned the true spirit of Christmas.

Introduction

Carol the glad tidings,
Carol merrily.

Kate Douglas Wiggin

It is good to be children sometimes, and never better than at Christmas, when its mighty Founder was a child himself.

Charles Dickens

Imagine sitting beside a crackling fire, quietly preparing for a festive and sacred Twelve Days of Christmas. This anthology helps you celebrate a soulful season of glad songs, from the dark stillness of Advent and Winter Solstice through Christmas, the New Year and Epiphany, on to the welcome light of a candle on a cold February night.

Advent means "coming" and is characterized by waiting in "Mary-darkness" or "Mary-space," like the pregnant Virgin awaiting the birth of her son. The humble donkey inspires an appropriate Advent pace. "I cannot heigh-ho, and ho! ho! / My way to Christmas Day!" writes poet Carol Crawford. "I want to stall my way to Christmas Day, / Lest I come, stranger to the Child, / Numb to the stable and the star."

Melanie McDonagh wrote "Don't Stop the Party" to encourage us to keep Advent simple and then celebrate the Twelve Days of Christmas in style. "Advent has been abolished," she writes, "and Christmas has been hideously elongated before it happens, yet truncated when it should be happening. The whole period of waiting for Christmas has been overtaken by the celebration of it."

When we prepare well with stillness and simplicity during Advent, we are ready to celebrate the full Twelve Days of Christmas, walking through a doorway on New Year's as a symbol of our new beginning, blessing gold, frankincense, and myrrh and marking the lintels of our front doors on Epiphany, blessing our homes and all who enter them in the coming year.

Does Jesus appreciate the Magi's exotic gifts or does he prefer the camel? How do the three gifts represent the contribution Hindus, Buddhists, and Muslims make to the world? What happens if you find a bean in the Twelfth Night cake you baked for the feast?

Season of Glad Songs includes rituals and prayers for lighting the Advent wreath and blessing New Year's calendars, for blessing each figure you place in your manger scene, for blessing candles on February 2, known as Candlemas, the fortieth day after the birth of Jesus and the traditional ending of the Christmas season.

We filled these pages with some of our favorite seasonal meditations, charming black and white illustrations by a variety of artists, and both original and familiar poems. We recommend books, movies, and music to enjoy alone or with your family and friends during this rich season.

Our selections range from Caroline Kennedy's *A Family Christmas* and Patrick Stewart's incomparable role as Ebenezer Scrooge to *How the Hollyhocks Came to New Mexico*; from Paul Horn's tranquil *Peace Album* to Smokey Robinson's rock 'n' roll version of "We Three Kings of Orient Are" with a rousing cheer at the end ("Gimme a J!"); from the spiritual wisdom of Thomas Merton and St. Thérèse to Christmas customs around the world, foods and feasting, folklore and legends about the Christmas tree and candy canes, wassail and rosemary. (Why are the flowers blue?)

Lest we become overly sentimental at Christmastime and forget the broken world in which we live, we include Alfred Delp's prison insights into the "terror" of Christmas by Sharon Doyle, Winston Churchill's stirring greetings from the White House as the U.S. was about to enter World War II, and the paradox of "merriment in a warring world."

In the words of British author Caryll Houselander, we must change "the round, sorrowful world to a cradle for God" and "be hands that are rocking the world to a kind rhythm of love: that the incoherence of war and the chaos of unrest be soothed to a lullaby."

We hope there's something here for everyone, young or old, whether you follow the Christian path, an interspiritual one, or none at all, since Christmas entwines both the sacred and the secular. *Season of Glad Songs* is our joyful gift to all of you: "Glad Tidings we bring, to you and your friends. We wish you a Merry Christmas and a Happy New Year!"

—*Tessa Bielecki and David Denny*
Advent 2013

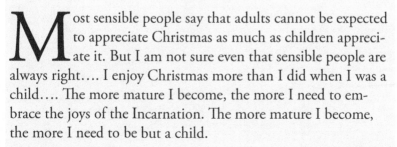

Most sensible people say that adults cannot be expected to appreciate Christmas as much as children appreciate it. But I am not sure even that sensible people are always right…. I enjoy Christmas more than I did when I was a child…. The more mature I become, the more I need to embrace the joys of the Incarnation. The more mature I become, the more I need to be but a child.

G.K. Chesterton

Part 1

Advent

I live my Advent in the womb of Mary....
  I knew for long she carried me and fed me,
Guarded and loved me, though I could not see.
    But only now, with inward jubilee,
I come upon earth's most amazing knowledge:
  Someone is hidden in this dark with me.

Jessica Powers

Rejoice, rejoice, O Israel,
To you shall come Emmanuel.
Traditional Carol

Advent is a season of inner transformation that

mirrors changes in the outer landscape. Fields lie fallow. The days grow darker. Winter, the season of death, approaches.

In his seminal book, *Transitions*, William Bridges describes the phases of change we experience in our lives: "First there is an ending, then a beginning, with an important empty or fallow time in between. That is the order of things in nature." Advent is the "important empty or fallow time" in between the ending of the Christian liturgical year and the birth of Jesus, symbol of our own rebirth, and a whole new beginning.

Advent is permeated by darkness and then the coming of light. How can we be at home in the darkness and wait in fallow emptiness and expectation like the pregnant Mary of Nazareth? Instead of celebrating Christmas too early and collapsing on December 25, I try to slow down, simplify, and cultivate the spirit of leisure during Advent. Then I'm ready to celebrate the full Twelve Days of Christmas.

Enhance the season by lighting the Advent wreath every evening. Pray the "Oh Antiphons" and meditate on the "Animal Ohs." Commemorate the feast of Our Lady of Guadalupe, who communicates in flower and song. "Even if you don't own a donkey," Fr. Dave recommends a festive retelling of the story of Juan Diego and your own family procession.

"Sleep does not come easy this season," explains Dorothy McFarland in the seminal poem I've cherished every Advent since 1978. "This is the time of preparation," she says, encouraging us to be awake and watchful, not necessarily "super-cheerful."

Alfred Delp helps me counteract a superficial season of Advent with his realistic emphasis on hope in the midst of fear and terror. Though his hands were bound in chains inside a Nazi prison, he was able to wriggle one hand free enough to write his own Advent reflections, and smuggle them out inside his dirty laundry bag.

Yes, we need "images of tenderness, peace, and love," writes McFarland, but we can't "spring Christmas out of a hat like a magician's white rabbit...the real thing isn't a piece of stage craft...complete with real sheep and a donkey." We come to Christ's birth and our own rebirth through "a season of death we undergo."

—*Tessa Bielecki*

Underworld

David Denny

A way tunnels under the subway,
Scrapes true through the skull of the sky,
Bleeds life on the withering city,
Sets fire to the lingering lie.

Under the concrete empire,
Under the black-topped sod,
Dark in the womb of a virgin:
Heart of an unborn God.

Glad Tidings for Advent

Each year as Christmas draws near,
  We come, once more, to the Advent Door,
  To that Nazareth that whelms within—
  Mary-space, openness to grace...
  Carol Crawford

This is the irrational season
When love blooms bright and wild.
Had Mary been filled with reason
There'd have been no room for the child.
Madeleine L'Engle

Advent is the empty still season... If we keep Advent still and uncluttered, we will be awake and ready when Christ comes. He does not stick rigidly to our liturgical feast days. He may come December 4 or December 26.
William McNamara

Advent is the season of the seed...the season of the secret of Divine Love growing in silence.... Advent is essential to our contemplation, too.... We must not try to force Christ's growth in us, but with a deep gratitude for the light burning secretly in our darkness, we must fold our concentrated love upon him like earth, surrounding, holding, and nourishing the seed.
Caryll Houselander

Advent begins with a stirring call to "Awake!" It summons us to consciousness, inviting us to re-connect to the feminine aspect of the Self, to our feeling, to our kinship with the earth, the body, and sexual energies.
Mary Ann Burke, R.C.S.J.

I wait in Mary-darkness, faith's walled place, with hope's expectance of nativity.
Jessica Powers

Advent

The Mystery of Darkness and Light

Tessa Bielecki

"Descent into darkness" is an appropriate description of the meaning of Advent. As poet Dorothy McFarland wrote: "Every Advent, the same thing: the unwelcome descent into darkness, into the waste places of the soul, the abode of demons. The cold groping in the interior reaches of one's poverty." Notice how many dimensions of St. John of the Cross's Dark Night of the Soul are expressed here so poetically: unwelcome descent, darkness, waste places, demons, cold groping, interior poverty.

"Cold walk in the dark," another profound description of Advent, comes from musician Tom Renaud, who wrote: "The message of Christmas is not a bag of goodies but a cold walk in the dark. The story of the Nativity reveals that Jesus became flesh 'out there' in the cold. That is where the shepherds who left their warm fires to look for him found him. We, too, must leave behind whatever little fires are keeping us too warm and comfortable and seek Christ where he is to be found.... If taken seriously, prayer isn't a nice 'warm glow,' but becomes in a very real way an exposure to cold and dark." Another great description of the Dark Night of the Soul: leaving behind the warm glow of the little fires that keep us warm and comfortable and exposing ourselves to cold and dark.

> The Advent wreath is a potent symbol and Zen Christian koan or riddle. For how can we descend into darkness by lighting the candles of the wreath?

Both the season of Advent and the Dark Night of the Soul immerse us in the primordial mystery of darkness and light. "Primordial" is my favorite word. I not only love its meaning; I love the way the word becomes flesh in my mouth. The mystery of the Dark Night is so primordial, that is, so elementary, so basic, so fundamental, that long before we ever hear the name John of the Cross or learn about Carmelite spirituality, we encounter the reality of the Dark Night.

The sun sets. Night falls. The world descends into darkness and shadows appear. What did not concern us during the hours of daylight now become matters of terrible concern: the dark at the top of the stairs, the monster under the bed, childhood images of what Psalm 90 from the Jewish Testament calls the "terror of the night" or the "plague that prowls in the darkness."

Daydreams and Nightmares

Our night dreams are colored differently than our day dreams. Daydreams are usually every bright color of the rainbow, but night dreams are so black we call them "nightmares." Another great primordial word: nightmare. We understand nightmare as a bad dream that comes in the night, but it originally meant a monster or evil spirit that attacks us while we sleep. All of us know that having a nightmare often feels like being attacked by the boogeyman. In the traditional monastic prayer called Compline, the night prayer that "completes" the day, we sing: "Help and defend us through the night; danger and terror put to flight." Another old translation is more poetic, graphic, and more specific: "From evil dreams defend our eyes, from nightly fears and fantasies." Our primordial fear of the dark is at root our fear of death, dramatized at night because sleep resembles our experience of death.

Dying of the Light

In a charming novel I read years ago, the central character invited his friends in for a glass of wine every day at dusk, because, he said: "The coming of the dark is the foreshadowing of blindness and death and a time when it is not good for us to be alone." It seems, then, that the late afternoon cocktail hour in contemporary society is not merely a jolly social custom: it grows out of our primordial fear of the dark. Some people take tea at this time instead. For the same profound reason, Christian monks around the world gather to pray Vespers at dusk every day. Perhaps Dylan Thomas summed it up best when he said: "Do not go gently into the Dark Night, but rage, rage against the dying of the light."

Rejoicing at Dawn

John of the Cross, Doctor of the Church and one of my spiritual fathers, was not the first doctor or father to teach me about the Dark Night. I learned initially from my biological father, another kind of doctor: a family physician with a special interest in obstetrics and gynecology. I spent my childhood waking up in the night hearing the telephone, my father's muffled voice, and his car driving away to the hospital so he could deliver another baby. I also heard my father yell a lot at his patients in the night because they always seemed to complain of aches and pains more dramatically in the dark than in the daylight. There was deep significance in the patients' distress.

They were experiencing the primordial mystery of darkness and light, the mystery of life and death, expressed so magnificently in Psalm 29: "At nightfall, weeping enters in, but with the dawn rejoicing." The pain that can be so intense at night is far more bearable once morning comes. Psalm 29 is a good prayer first thing in the morning. It begins: "You brought me up from the nether world; you preserved me from among those going down into the pit." I am out of the nether world of night, the black hole, the void of darkness, the bowels of hell, "the abode of demons," and into the light of day.

Dayspring and Morning Star

The beautiful Canticle of Zachary concludes the monastic morning prayer we call Lauds. Zachary's song expresses the true spirit of the early morning hours: "In the tender compassion of our God, the dawn from on high shall break upon us, to shine on those who dwell in darkness and the shadow of death." After the terror of the night, when darkness has covered us like the shroud of death, the "dawn from on high" shines upon us. I love reflecting on different translations of "dawn from on high": dayspring, daystar, morning star, eastern star, Orient, rising sun, in the Christian tradition, all referring to Christ himself. Other traditional prayers at Lauds also lead to exultation: "At daybreak we were filled with your mercy. We rejoiced and were delighted." And: "This is the day which the Lord has made. Let us rejoice and be glad in it!"

It is natural to rejoice in the coming of the dawn, the coming of daybreak, the rising of the morning star. But according to John of the Cross, it is an even greater grace to rejoice in the darkness of the night, that guiding and glad night "more lovely than the dawn." Through the Carmelite tradition, fathered by the Doctor of the Dark Night, we learn to be more at peace and at home in the dark. Why? Because it is in that very dark, that very night, that Lover is united with beloved, "transforming the beloved in her Lover."

The Advent Wreath

Just as there is no way into the light of day except through the darkness of night, there is no way into the light of Christmas except through the darkness of Advent. Just as there is no way into the light of Easter except through the darkness of the tomb, there is no way into the light of Christmas except through the darkness of Mary's womb.

In the spirit of St. John of the Cross, we enter the season of Advent, a descent into the dark night, paradoxically by lighting the Advent wreath every evening. The Advent wreath is a potent Christian symbol and a magnificent Zen Christian *koan* or riddle, meant to shock us out of our mental ruts, shatter our comfortable rational concepts and awaken our mythic and poetic awareness. For how can we descend into darkness by lighting the candles of the Advent wreath?

In the simple primordial gesture of lighting the candles, we immerse ourselves in the ultimate mystery of darkness and light expressed so well in Psalm 138: "For you darkness itself is not dark, and night shines clear as day. Darkness and light are the same."

Making an Advent Wreath

Tessa Bielecki

Make a circular wreath of evergreens with three purple (or blue) candles and one rose (or pink). Light one purple candle at the beginning of the first, second, and fourth weeks of Advent. Light the rose candle at the beginning of the third week when we rejoice because Christ is coming very soon. The first word of the liturgy this third week is "Rejoice," so that Sunday is called Gaudete *Sunday. Each week meditate on one of our Advent reflections and pray this prayer:*

O Creator, by whose word all things are sanctified, pour forth your blessings upon this wreath. Keep us wakeful and help us prepare for Christ's coming. Give us the gifts of the Holy Spirit. Help us beat our swords into plows and pruning hooks and build a peaceful, fertile world, a world where the wolf and the lamb, the calf and the lion lie down in peace. May our desert bloom, and may we wait in patience for the Holy One, Emmanuel.

Two Poems for Advent

Dorothy McFarland

Sleep is never easy in this season
though the day grinds down
the mind to numbness
and blinds the eye
to signs and portents
Still the pulse wobbles
uneasily in the neck
and the heart pounds in its hollow cage
like a door banged in the wind.

Sleep is never easy in this season.
This is the time of Preparation;
We are commanded to be watchful.
Do we imagine we await a smiling
Mother
and a radiant Child?

Why, then,
does my heart boom
in the hollow halls of my house
and my bones shudder
as if under the tread
of some dark thief
in the night?

II
I feel like Cassandra, seeing blood
in the streets
When everyone else is being supercheerful
Or a skeletal John the Baptist, *metanoeite*
blazed across my chest,
an embarrassment at a banquet.

They've changed the liturgical colors
from purple for penance to blue
(less heavy trip)
but blue will do for me as well—
the color of cold steel
that pierces me like the eyes of the priest
communing me
—*alter Christus*—
to sound my heart and gizzard
lay bare my prophetic guts
Prepare the way of the Lord.
Make his way straight.
Every Advent, the same thing:
the unwelcome descent into darkness,
into the waste places of the soul,
the abode of demons.
The cold groping in the interior reaches of
one's poverty,
The paralysis of the will that stares in
dismay
at massive irrational stones.
For God's sake, don't spring Christmas
out of a hat
like a magician's white rabbit—
God knows we need what we conjure,
images of tenderness, peace, love.
But the real thing isn't a piece
of stagecraft
however lifelike, complete with
real sheep
and a donkey.
We come to Christ's birth
not as actors in a pageant
but through a season of death
we undergo.

2

Flower and Song

Guadalupe, the New Eve

David Denny

The first time I heard the story of Our Lady of Guadalupe, I was twenty-one, considering monastic life, and about to be confirmed a Roman Catholic. A beloved Sedona, Arizona neighbor, Mary Brodie, was bedridden with rheumatoid arthritis, and a friend and I visited her at her little home up nearby Jack's Canyon. Mary had an image of Our Lady of Guadalupe, and when I told her I didn't know the story, she launched in. Mary told stories beautifully. I remember being taken by the tale, but this Marian stuff was foreign to me.

The more I learned about the sixteenth-century apparition to the Indian Juan Diego in Mexico, the more I quietly fell in love with the details. Two dozen years later, I had become a monk and my community decided to celebrate the Feast of Our Lady of Guadalupe with greater solemnity. This translated into an outdoor procession with our donkey Lupe!

Mother of the New Creation

In preparation for the feast, I read Virgil Elizondo's *Guadalupe: Mother of the New Creation* and was struck by the creatively subversive, revolutionary aspect of the Virgin's appearance. In case you don't know the tale, here it is: In 1531, Juan Diego, a native living near Mexico City, left home before dawn on his way to church. He heard some extraordinary music, like beautiful birdsong, coming from above him on the hill of Tepeyac. Then he heard himself addressed. He climbed the hill and met a beautiful lady who asked him to deliver a message to the bishop: she wanted the bishop to build her a "hermitage," a chapel, on this hill sacred to the natives. Juan reluctantly went to the bishop's palace, where he was peremptorily dismissed.

Juan returned to the lady, reported his failure and suggested she find a better messenger. She sent him back. After a thorough interview, the bishop dismissed Juan a second time, insisting he needed a sign that would confirm the truth of Juan's outlandish claim.

> The Aztec symbols on Mary's robe announced the dawning of a new age with an infant sun.

Dejected, Juan returned home to find his uncle gravely ill. So the next day, before dawn, he headed to Mexico City to get a priest. He skirted the hill to avoid the lady. But she saw and intercepted him. She assured him that his uncle was already cured and told him to climb the hill and pick the flowers he would find there. It was December 12. He found the impossible Castilian flowers, filled his mantle, or *tilma,* with them, and brought them to the lady, who sent him on to the palace.

There he met a cold reception and waited a long time. Finally the bishop saw him. Juan knelt and told his tale. He opened his *tilma* and out poured the flowers. But they were nothing compared to the lightning bolt that struck the bishop: the emptied *tilma* bore a radiant image of the beautiful lady. The bishop was converted.

An Indigenous Mother

Elizondo's commentary places this event in its historical context and illuminates details that cannot be recounted here, heightening the tale's drama. He describes some of the Aztec background of the story. Although the Spaniards brought the

Christian faith, the lady made it clear that the indigenous Mexicans were the Spaniards' equals. Elizondo sees the Virgin's message as a mandate for missionaries that would not be fully embraced by the Church until recently, with teachings renouncing evangelization through destruction of native cultures. The timing for this intervention was uncanny. The conquest of Mexico began in 1519. By 1531, the native population was devastated by warfare, disease, and persecution.

The Virgin's features and dress were Aztec, not Spanish. This was unprecedented. Elizondo describes the Aztec hieroglyphic symbols on Mary's robe; illiterate natives may have been able to "read" the message encoded there: a new age, with an infant sun, had dawned. No one knows why the *tilma* has not disintegrated after four and a half centuries, and no one knows how the haunting image was made. Even if and when natural causes are discovered to account for these anomalies, how can we account for the miracle of the message, the flower and song of its truth?

Earthy Mysticism

I love the earthiness of Christian mysticism and the warm humanity of Jesus. Rather than "intervening" in a "godless" situation, it seems more accurate to me that God is already present, working from within the creation God loves, and especially through human instruments. But when innocent people are oppressed, God sometimes seems to erupt in a dramatic way, perhaps especially when it requires challenging authorities for the sake of the poor, the underdogs and outcasts. Aztec sages claimed that truth is always clothed in *flor y canto*, flower and song. The heavenly music and the presence of flowers at the crest of Tepeyac in December are not only, and perhaps not mainly, miracles, but rather a confirmation that what was revealed there was true.

In our celebration of Our Lady of Guadalupe, we decked our donkey Lupe with paper flowers, and we attached a New

Mexican *santo* carving of the Virgin on Lupe's packsaddle. Beginning at our garage, we processed about a quarter of a mile down our gravel road to Lupe's corral. When the feast fell on a Sunday, we invited neighbor children to join us. They strewed dried flower petals in front of Lupe as we sang our way to the corral. Once there, we started a campfire and read the Guadalupe story aloud.

> We decked our donkey Lupe with paper flowers and put a New Mexican santo on her packsaddle.

When we reached the climactic moment when Juan Diego opens his flower-filled *tilma*, we unfolded a brightly colored Mexican blanket that hung on the corral fence. Paper and felt roses tumbled out on the ground, revealing a poster of Our Lady of Guadalupe. It is a child-like ceremony, more like a grammar school skit than a grand liturgical drama. But in the chilly December light, as the sun set over the San Juan Mountains, I felt profound gratitude. Sometimes we lingered fireside with hot chocolate or adjourned to the dining room for a meal of *huevos rancheros*.

Just because you don't have a donkey doesn't mean you can't celebrate this feast! And in the midst of reveling, it is good to remember the source of our joy. The New World, says Elizondo, gave birth to a new race, the *mestizos*, once shunned by both European and native cultures. Our Lady of Guadalupe proclaims herself their mother, our mother. She is the New World's New Eve, mother of a diverse human ecology that rejects the monocultures of European imperialist *hubris* and Aztec human sacrifice, subordinating them to *flor y canto*, the liberating truth and celebration of God's love here and now.

Freedom in Prison

Alfred Delp's Advent Hope

Sharon Doyle

The Prison Meditations of Father Delp with an introduction by Thomas Merton rank as one of the great human and spiritual documents of our time, full of honesty and sincerity. They contain the thoughts of a man trapped by a mendacious system. Alfred Delp, a German Jesuit, refused to accept the Nazi regime and joined a secret anti-Nazi group which met to plan a new social order based on the Gospel. He was arrested for treason and executed on February 2, 1945. In his last letter he wrote: "The actual reason for my condemnation was that I happened to be and chose to remain a Jesuit."

As he paced his narrow prison cell and faced certain death, Delp clung to the hope given us in the revelation of the Incarnation: our God is with us. According to Merton, it was in solitude, loneliness, helplessness, emptiness, and desperation that Delp *experienced* Truth. It is striking that these prison meditations are permeated with both realism and hope. With a prophetic voice Delp articulates conditions fatal to humankind and asks:

> *What are all the lessons learned through our suffering and misery if no bridge can be thrown from our side to the other shore? What is the point of our fear if it brings no enlightenment and does not penetrate the darkness and dispel it? What use is it shuddering at the world's coldness if we cannot discover the grace to conjure up better conditions?*

One of the terrors inherent in a prophetic vocation is the vision of evil within and without. Delp faced the treachery of his times; he faced himself and what humanity is capable of. So must we. He accepted the desolation his vision brought him. So must we. This kind of acceptance leads to a vision of redemption and to the theological virtue of Hope, a great flaming torch compared to the flickerings of our merely human hopes.

> Unless a man has been shocked to his depths at himself and the things he is capable of, as well as the failings of humanity as a whole, he cannot understand the full import of Advent.

Melting the Deep Ice

This dark vision forces us into the proper dispositions for Advent and prepares us for the Light who comes into the darkness of our world. Darkness *cannot* overpower the Light. Delp wrote from experience: "Unless a man has been shocked to his depths at himself and the things he is capable of, as well as the failings of humanity as a whole, he cannot understand the full import of Advent." Our little hopes have to be smashed before we can appreciate our need for Hope. Delp noticed that before he went to prison he used to mouth the words *hope* and *trust* glibly, as we all tend to do, until we surrender to deeper levels of being. In prison, his prayers for love and life melted the ice deep within him. In darkness he learned to take seriously God's command to trust absolutely and wholeheartedly. When he had lost everything and faced physical death, Delp learned that God alone suffices. God is enough. But before God is enough for us, most of us need to be shattered and awakened. In these poignant meditations, Delp insists that life begins only when our whole framework is shaken.

> We have not grasped what Delp calls the terror and the beauty of Advent and Christmas. When we live out of this reality, the morning star, the Light of Christ, rises in our hearts.

The Terror and Beauty of Christmas

Over two thousand years ago, God became human in a brand new way. We still haven't begun to grasp the significance of this action. We have not grasped what Delp calls the terror and the beauty of Advent and Christmas. By waiting in prayer, suffering, and affliction, we begin expanding our capacity for the truth that God-is-with-us and we are loved. When we live out of this reality, the morning star, the Light of Christ, has risen in our minds and hearts. This kind of vision changes the world. In spite of the chaos around him, Alfred Delp lived and died in Hope, which he expressed gloriously in these words: "Even this shambles in which we now live, this devastation, is the destined place and hour of a new holy night, a new birth for humanity seeking God, a new nativity. Darkness shall not frighten us or distress wear us out; we will go on waiting, watching and praying until the star rises."

"Darkness shall
not frighten us or
distress wear us
out; we will go on
waiting, watching
and praying until
the star rises."

Fr. Delp

3

The Oh Antiphons

Primordial Praise-Names

Tessa Bielecki

One of the richest Christian traditions is the praying of the "Oh Antiphons" on the seven days before Christmas. We learn to appreciate these Antiphons more deeply if we take a closer look at theology, anthropology and even twentieth-century American musical-comedy.

The "Oh" of Ecstasy

I've loved Broadway musicals since I was a young girl. My favorite is *The Fantastiks,* the longest running musical in American history. I saw it for the fifth time recently in a tiny off-Broadway theater and marveled at how much more I understood since the first time I saw it in my early twenties. *The Fantastiks* is essentially a story about the movement from romance to mysticism. (There are tremendous similarities between Broadway musicals and Christian mysticism, but this is not the place to explore that fascinating topic.)

The heroine of *The Fantastiks* is a terribly romantic and naive sixteen-year-old girl. In one of the opening scenes she screams "Oh!" almost a hundred times and falls into a swoon: "Oh, oh, oh!... I hug myself till my arms turn blue and my tears come down and I can taste them!" The girl is experiencing what poet Richard Wilbur calls the "oh of ecstasy." The word "oh" occurs over and over again in the writings of the Christian mystics.

The seven Oh Antiphons are "ohs of ecstasy," cries of the heart, cries of rapture, awe, wonder, mystery, and adoration. As Pierre Teilhard de Chardin, S.J., the French paleontologist-mystic, said: "The more human we become, the more we become prey to a need, a need...to adore." According to British author G.K. Chesterton, "If we cannot pray, we are gagged. If we cannot kneel, we are in chains."

In the Christian mystical tradition, adoration is the highest form of prayer. When we hear the "Good News" proclaimed by the Incarnation, The-Word-Made-Flesh we celebrate at Christmas, the good news expressed in every one of the Oh Antiphons, we may need to fall on our knees and adore, or hug ourselves till our arms turn blue and the tears come down and we can taste them. Full of mystery and awe, we wonder: How can this be true? It really is a dream come true.

"Praise-Names" from the African Bushmen

The Bushmen who live in the Kalahari Desert of southwest Africa are inherently religious. For these people, all life is sacred, holy, full of the Divine. So the Bushmen are full of gratitude and continually give praise.

They have "praise-names" for everything. Praise-names for people are similar to our "nicknames." But unlike our nicknames, Bushmen praise-names are not casual, irreverent or short. They are longer names, more sublime, and majestic. For example, the name *uLangalibalela,* given to a man who is "both a doctor of the body and healer of fading shadows," mysteriously means "The Right Honorable Sun-Is-Hot."

The Bushmen also give praise-names to the commonplace materials of their ordinary quotidian existence: to the spears, arrows, and other objects they use every day in order to survive in the harshness of their desert environment. A hunting spear may be called *U-Simsela-Banta-Bami*: "He-Digs-Up-For-My-Children" and a hunting club *Igumgehle*: "The-Greedy-One."

Like the African praise-names for *Umkulunkulu,* who is "the first spirit of all things," the Oh Antiphons are praise-names for the Holy One who "comes" to us on Christmas.

Primordial Words

Most of the Oh Antiphons are titles for the Messiah taken from the Jewish Testament. But it would be a mistake to see the origin of these antiphons in our Hebrew ancestors. The Oh Antiphons are older than ancient Israel: they grow out of our very bones, our blood, out of the depths of the human heart. The praise-names sung in the Oh Antiphons are as old as the awakening of human life on earth, which may be why they move us so deeply.

This is explained by German Jesuit Karl Rahner, whose work reflects the complementarity of theology and poetry. Rahner, who died in 1984, wrote eloquently about "primordial words":

There are words which delimit and isolate, but there are also words which render a single thing translucent to the infinity of all reality. They are like seashells, in which can be heard the sound of the ocean of infinity, no matter how small they are in themselves. They bring light to us, not we to them. They have power over us, because they are gifts of God, not [human] creations.... Some words are clear because they are shallow and without mystery; they suffice for the mind; by means of them one acquires mastery over things. Other words are perhaps

23

obscure because they evoke the blinding mystery of things. They pour out of the heart and sound forth in hymns. They open the doors to great works and they decide over eternities. Such words, which spring up from the heart, which hold us in their power, which enchant us, the glorifying, heaven-sent words, I should like to call primordial *words.*

What, then, are these "ohs of ecstasy," these praise-names, primordial words that Rahner says "evoke the blinding mystery of things?" These enchanting, "glorifying, heaven-sent words" which "spring up from the heart and hold us in their power... like seashells in which can be heard the sound of the ocean of infinity?" The Oh Antiphons are small words, signifying such tiny physical realities: key, root, star. Yet these tiny finite words open the door to infinity.

The Seven Antiphons

Here is the traditional translation of the seven antiphons. December 17: Oh Wisdom. December 18: Oh Adonai. December 19: Oh Root of Jesse. December 20: Oh Key of David. December 21: Oh Dayspring. December 22: Oh King. December 23: Oh Emmanuel. These are the images we sing in the verses of the traditional Advent hymn, "O Come Emmanuel."

What is the origin and meaning of the seven Oh Antiphons? The Wisdom books of the Jewish Testament prefigure Jesus, the Word of God. Christians believe that Jesus was active in Jewish Testament history as Adonai or the "Covenant of God." In the Book of Revelation, St. John refers to Jesus as the Key of David, borrowing from Isaiah.

Isaiah, too, is the source for the Root of Jesse: "There shall come forth a shoot out of the root of Jesse, and a flower shall rise up out of his root." Jesse was King David's father, and Jesus is the Son of David. Chronologically, Jesus came after David, and so is called the Flower of Jesse's Stem. But ontologically he came before David, so he is called the Root of Jesse. Jesus is Alpha and Omega, the beginning and the end.

In Christian scripture and liturgy, the Radiant Dawn, Morning Star, Sun of Justice, or Dayspring from on High are all used as symbols for Christ. Both Jewish and Christian Testament references are numerous, including Zachariah 3:8 and 6:12, Malachy 4:2, Wisdom 7:26, Hebrews 1:3, and Luke 1:78-79.

When we pray the sixth antiphon, O King and Cornerstone, we have a problem, despite references in Isaiah, Ephesians, and Matthew. There is not one cornerstone in a building, but four. So it may be more appropriate to call Jesus the Keystone, since there is only one keystone in an arch. And Jesus is the Desire of Nations, the Keystone uniting Jew and Gentile, binding two into one.

"Oh Come"

In the traditional prayers said on the first Sunday of Advent, the most important and most primordial word is *come*: "Oh Lord, rouse up your power and come." After Vatican II, Church officials rewrote the Oh Antiphons and unfortunately eliminated the word *Oh*. But they saw fit to place emphasis instead on the word *come*, which begins each of their late twentieth-century translations of the seven antiphons.

The symbolism of the seven Oh Antiphons is vivid and dramatic. The key, the root, and the dayspring (star or rising sun) are obvious. Several of the other symbols are less evident. Wisdom is usually depicted by the all-seeing eye of God or a

> The seven Oh Antiphons are "ohs of ecstasy," cries of the heart, cries of rapture, awe, wonder, mystery, and adoration. They grow out of the depths of the human heart.

scroll and Adonai, Ruler of Ancient Israel, by a Jewish star, the burning bush, or the Ten Commandments.

Creating your own Oh Antiphons out of paper, fabric, or wood is a wonderful way to celebrate the season of Advent. When I lived in monastic community, we began first with paper and hung the symbols up one by one as we prayed the Antiphon for each day. But paper was too flimsy. The next year we made them out of purple cloth filled with pinto beans. But the beans were too heavy, and all the antiphons crashed to the floor. The following year we stuffed them with pampers left behind by one of our guests with a baby, but this was too cumbersome.

> Primordial words are like seashells, in which can be heard the sound of the ocean of infinity.

We finally carved our antiphons out of wood and painted them bright colors. Our anticipation of Christ's coming was greatly enhanced each Advent season as the familiar wooden patterns were hung secretly each night in the chapel. Forty years later, I have my own personal set of wooden antiphons and put one out in my hermitage on each one of these seven special days.

It is impossible to absorb the mystery and majesty revealed in the Oh Antiphons simply by reading about them. You must pray the Antiphons, or their "magic" will not work. And they must be prayed not merely once but over and over, day after day, year after year, until they permeate your entire being.

For your Advent enrichment, you will find my own translation of the Oh Antiphons on the following pages. May each one plunge you ever more deeply into the inexhaustible mystery of the Word-Made-Flesh we celebrate at Christmas.

Praying the Oh Antiphons

This version of the "Oh Antiphons" by Tessa Bielecki combines several ancient translations. It is meant to be prayed aloud by a chorus of at least two voices, although it can also be prayed alone. In addition to the seven traditional prayers, Christ the Tiger and Christ the Lightning-Dynamite are included, inspired by T.S. Eliot and Thomas Merton. You may want to write more Oh Antiphons of your own, based on your own experience.

Praying the
Oh Antiphons

Tessa Bielecki

1. Oh Wisdom

2. Oh Wisdom

1. & 2. Oh Wisdom of our God Most High!

1. You reach from beginning to end and order all things with gentleness and strength, guiding creation with power and love. Come!

2. Come!

1. & 2. Come and teach us to walk in the way of truth.

1. Oh Adonai

2. Oh Lord and Leader

1. & 2. Oh Ruler of Ancient Israel!

1. You appeared to Moses in the fire of the burning bush and on Mount Sinai you gave him your law. Come!

2. Come!

1. & 2. Come and rescue us with your mighty outstretched arm.

1. Oh Root of Jesse

2. Oh Flower of Jesse's stem

1. & 2. Oh Flower of Jesse's stem!

1. You are a sign of God's love for all peoples. Before you kings shall keep silence. Come!

2. Come!

1. & 2. Come and save us without delay.

1. Oh Key of David

2. Oh Key of David

1. & 2. Oh Key of David and Sceptre of the House of Israel!

1. You open and no one closes. You close and no one opens. Come!

2. Come!

1. & 2. Come and free us from the prison of darkness.

1. Oh Radiant Dawn

2. Oh Morning Star

1. & 2. Oh Dayspring from on High!

1. In the tender compassion of our God, Come!

2. Come!

1. & 2. Come and enlighten those who dwell in the shadow of death.

1. Oh King of all peoples

2. Oh Desired of all nations

1. & 2. Oh Source of all unity and faith!

1. You are the Keystone uniting Jew and Gentile, binding two into one. Come!

2. Come!

1. & 2. Come and deliver all peoples, whom you fashioned out of clay.

I. Oh King and Lawgiver

2. Oh long-awaited Savior of the nations

1. & 2. Oh Emmanuel, God's Presence among us!

1. Come!

2. Come!

1. & 2. Come and save us, Lord our God.

1. Oh Word within a Word

2. Oh Word within a Word

1. & 2. Oh Word within a Word!

1. You are swaddled with darkness. In the juvescence of the year, Come!

2. Come!

1. & 2. Come, Christ the Tiger! *(from T.S. Eliot)*

1. Make ready for the Christ

2. Make ready for the Christ

1. & 2. Make ready for the Christ

1. Whose smile like lightning sleeps in your paper flesh

2. Sleeps in your paper flesh

1. & 2. Sleeps in your paper flesh like dynamite!
   (from Thomas Merton)

4

A Christian Bestiary

Animals in Our Souls

David Denny

*W*hat does a kiss mean? It means one thing to a baby, something else to a bride, and something different to Judas. We might call a kiss a depth symbol. Depth symbols are not literal. They are fraught with connotations, allusions, memory, emotion, mystery, history. They're more like chords than single notes. They don't mean simply one thing. But sometimes we need clarity. So we also employ efficiency symbols, useful timesavers. They communicate quickly and unambiguously. A stop sign is a good example.

Depth symbols do not develop overnight but over generations. They may be lost, corrupted or eclipsed. If so, should we recover them? How? We can begin by remembering our cultural heritage and recapturing stories of our faith. Stories and legacies may be lost to our conscious minds, but they linger in our souls. We do not want to turn the clock back to the Middle Ages, but revisiting the past can give us a glimpse of some valuables we may have lost along our way.

In the thirteenth century, Christianity and European culture formed a synthesis. Sacred and profane intermingled, for better and worse. Symbols expanded. In European art, paintings of the life of Christ and Mary are full of symbols that people shared and understood. Later, in the secular art of the Unicorn Tapestries, woven around 1500, dozens of plants and animals appear as symbols for virtues and vices, with the unicorn a symbol for Christ.

A Taste of Wonder

As far back as the fourth or even the second century, a collection of animal legends called the *Physiologus* became popular and captured the imagination of later generations. The Middle Ages compiled animal legends that told more about Christ than about the animals themselves. In that spirit, let's look at some symbols of Christ that may help your prayer, or at least entertain you and lure you into the leisurely realm of youthful imagination. The childlike enter the Kingdom, and children live in the world of symbol. "We are coming today to understand

> What does a kiss mean? It means one thing to a baby, something else to a bride, and something different to Judas.

something of which the nineteenth century could have had no idea: that symbol, myth, image belong to the very substance of the psychic life; that you can camouflage them, mutilate or degrade them, but never extirpate them," according to historian of religions Mircea Eliade.

Symbolic thinking "is consubstantial with the human being, preceding language and discursive reason. The symbol reveals certain aspects of reality—the deepest aspects—which defy all other modes of knowledge." The atrocities of our age may be "due in great part to a growing sterilization of the imagination." Or maybe our imaginations are not so much sterilized as "down-sized" to include only militaristic myths of demonization and materialist myths of ever-more wealth and consumption. Rich symbols or even simplistic allegories can be a respite, a taste of wonder in such a shrunken milieu.

These suggestions are an odd egghead introduction to a queer and quaint list of saintly beasts. Just keep this in mind: in their caves some thirty thousand years ago, our ancestors drew and painted splendid animal images, as you can see in the extraordinary film *Cave of Forgotten Dreams*. Our progenitors seem to have revered the creatures who fed, clothed, sheltered them, and provided them with materials for tools and weapons. We owe them our lives.

Dogs of God

Dogs teach us to be faithful. They may have been domesticated fifty thousand years ago! We were a great team: human eyes and wit united to canine nose and speed. According to the twelfth-century *Cambridge Bestiary*,

> *none is more sagacious than the Dog, for he has more perception than other animals and he alone recognizes his own name. He esteems his Master highly... the house-dogs look after the palisade of their masters, lest it should be robbed in the night by thieves, and these will stand up for their owners to the death.*

Homer's *Odyssey* includes a touching dog story. After twenty years away from home, Odysseus returns, incognito, to drive out his wife's suitors. Disguised as a beggar, he approaches his beloved dwelling and speaks with his companion.

> *A dog lying near lifted his head and ears. Argos it was, the dog of hardy Odysseus, whom long ago he reared but never used. Before the dog was grown, Odysseus went to sacred Ilios.... Now Argos lay neglected, his master gone away, upon the pile of dung which had been dropped before the door by mules*

*and oxen, and which lay there in a heap for slaves
to carry off and dung the broad lands of Odysseus.
Here lay the dog, this Argos, full of fleas. Yet even
now, seeing Odysseus near, he wagged his tail and
dropped both ears, but toward his master he had not
strength to move. Odysseus turned aside and wiped
away a tear.*

For safety's sake, Odysseus had to maintain his role as a
stranger and could not acknowledge the dog. "He entered the
stately house and went straight down the hall among the lordly
suitors. But upon Argos fell the doom of darksome death when
he beheld Odysseus, twenty years away."

A Heartbroken Swan

We don't always have to look to Homer or the Middle
Ages for animal allegories. In *The Cowboy and the Cossack* by
Clair Huffaker, we meet another model of fidelity: the swan.
A young American cowboy travels across Siberia with a herd
of cattle, some compatriot cowboys, and a troop of Cossacks.
Rostov, the Cossack leader, is far more sophisticated than the
Americans. The boy, Levi, rides alongside Rostov one day and
spots two beautiful swans high overhead "crossing gracefully
under the lowering sun." Rostov takes time to describe to Levi
the swans' attributes.

*They choose a mate when they're very young.
And they stay together for all the rest of their lives....*

*When I first came out east to Siberia, I was just
a youngster, about your age. That's when I saw my
first pair of them....*

*We'd been out hunting, and we'd made camp
near the end of the day, when two swans flew overhead. The other men were also new to the country,
and one of them grabbed his gun and shot the female
of the swans. It fell almost at our feet, dead.... All that*

*night the male swan flew overhead, circling the camp
in the dark, never landing anywhere to rest, and crying pitifully in its low, keening way for some answer
from its mate. I've never heard cries more pleading,
more terribly sad.... The next morning, it continued
to circle high over us, still in its own soft, searching
way, making those tragic, weeping sounds.... Then at
noon, with the sun nearly directly above us, the swan
finally lost all hope. It flew up and up, as high and as
far as its weakened wings would take it into the sky.
And then that great bird simply folded its wings and
plummeted down like a stone to smash itself to death
on the earth far below.... It had done the one thing it
possibly could do to rejoin its mate.*

The Bleeding Pelican

The pelican is a symbol of self-sacrifice or sorrowful wit-
ness. Christian churches sometimes include paintings or mosa-
ics depicting a pelican piercing its breast in order to feed its
blood to its hungry nestlings. Medieval bestiaries described the
pelican as an Egyptian bird whose offspring lash out at their
parents. Like fairy tales, some of these legends were not cute.
They included harrowing violence and convey theological atti-
tudes many no longer accept. In the pelican tale, the adults end
up killing the ungrateful and gluttonous chicks as punishment.
But after three days, they take pity, spill their own blood into the
chicks' beaks, and the chicks rise from death.

We may reject the wrath-and-punishment theme, but the
image of a parent giving life-blood to nourish offspring still
speaks to me, as does the Eucharist, in which Christ's body and
blood nourishes, heals, and transforms us.

The Lamb of God

The most frequently mentioned animal in the Christian
Testament is the lamb. One word, *amnos,* is used four times,

and each time it refers to Christ. The word *arnion* occurs thirty times, and on twenty-eight occasions refers to Christ. Only Jesus uses this word to refer to others. He sends his disciples out "like lambs among wolves," and tells Peter to "feed my lambs." The rest of the uses are all in Revelation. Since the image of the sacrificial lamb is so familiar, I want to suggest a different image for the Christ of Revelation, one that complements the Lamb and distances Jesus from mere victimhood.

> The Middle Ages compiled animal legends that told more about Christ than the animals themselves.

The Ram of God

In Revelation 13:11, the author describes a beast which "had two horns like a lamb." Maybe the writer is thinking of wild sheep rather than domestic. So the resurrected Lamb becomes the Ram, leader of the herd. As the ram fights the wolf and vanquishes him, so Christ battles with Satan and is victorious. The ram, the animal Abraham found in a thorny bush and sacrificed in place of his son Isaac, represents Christ crowned with thorns and sacrificed for us.

I imagine a bighorn ram when I read, "Next in my vision I saw Mount Zion and standing on it a Ram" and "Alleluia! The reign of the Lord our God Almighty has begun; let us be glad and rejoice and give praise to God, because this is the time for the marriage of the Ram."

The Yearning Stag

The stag can be a symbol both for Christ and for his followers, who pray, "like the deer that yearns for running streams, so my soul is yearning for you, my God."

A collection of medieval writings on the lives of the saints

35

recounts the conversion and life of St. Eustace, who encounters Christ in a stag. Before his conversion, Eustace was "master of the chivalry of Trajan, the emperor." He was a good man, but was not Christian. While hunting one day, he spied the most beautiful stag in a herd of deer. The stag darted into dense forest and Eustace pursued alone. The stag climbed onto a high rock and Eustace considered how he might get a good shot. As he studied the stag, Eustace "saw between his horns the form of the holy cross shining more clear than the sun." Jesus spoke to Eustace through the stag's mouth: "Wherefore followest me hither?... I am Jesu Christ, whom thou honourest ignorantly... and therefore I come hither so that by this hart that thou huntest I may hunt thee."

The legend of eighth-century Belgian St. Hubert tells a similar conversion tale. After his wife's death, Hubert spent all his time hunting until one Good Friday, he encountered a stag:

> *Hubert sallied forth to the chase. As he was pursuing a magnificent stag or hart, the animal turned and, as the pious legend narrates, he was astounded at perceiving a crucifix standing between its antlers, while he heard a voice saying: "Hubert, unless thou turnest to the Lord, and leadest an holy life, thou shalt quickly go down into hell."*

Like Eustace, Hubert indeed became a Christian and went on to become a bishop. He is the patron saint of hunters, and you can find an image of Hubert's cross on the label of *Jagermeister,* an herb-infused liqueur marketed as an ideal drink for hunters coming in from the cold.

In *The Spiritual Canticle,* St. John of the Cross says it is "characteristic of the stag to climb to high places and when wounded to race in search of refreshment and cool waters. If he hears the cry of his mate and senses that she is wounded, he immediately runs to her to comfort and coddle her."

Just for fun, here's a little digression: In monastic literature, animals are not always symbols. Some legends describe close relationships between holy men and women and wild beasts. I wish I were as fortunate as the Irish hermit St. Cainnic. When he wanted to read, a stag would come to his hermitage, lie down and hold the monk's book in his antlers!

Tyger! Tyger!

In an interview introducing Archbishop Anthony Bloom's classic *Beginning to Pray,* Bloom says, "to meet God is to enter into the 'cave of a tiger'—it is not a pussy cat you meet—it is a tiger. The [divine] realm...is dangerous. You must enter into it and not just seek information about it." Awe of the Adonai of Abraham, Isaac, Jacob, and Jesus is the beginning of wisdom. The Spirit is love, but this love can feel feral because it harrows the ego. In T. S. Eliot's *Gerontion,* an old man expresses the "thoughts of a dry brain in a dry season." The poem is full of images of decay, apathy, and the vanity of life. But twice the poem gives us sparks of light and life:

> *The word within a word, unable to speak a word,*
> *Swaddled with darkness. In the juvescence of the year*
> *Came Christ the tiger.*
> *The tiger springs in the new year. Us he devours.*

Christ consumes us with love and transforms us into himself. What mystery can compare with this? The Creator approaches as both lamb and tiger, and we stand in awe:

> *Tyger! Tyger! burning bright*
> *In the forests of the night,*
> *What immortal hand or eye*
> *Could frame thy fearful symmetry?*
>
> *...Did he who made the Lamb make thee?*
> —William Blake

Animal Oh Antiphons

David Denny

O mighty RAM, enthroned atop Mount Zion, guide us to your dwelling. By your strength we strive and by your blood we conquer dragons. Come, O victim-victor, bridegroom-ram, thou who art the great I AM.

O SALMON, leap like lightning from the womb, burst above cascades of chaos, climb love's deadly ladder; sow your blood and burning water at the ancient source of all our sorrow. Drowning, you destroy our death, leaping, you lead us to life. O ICHTHYS, come in glory.

O UNICORN, feral, fierce, and virile Lord, yet tender, soft, surrendered lover: pierce and purify us. Come, fleet steed of starlight, Prince of Dreams, Horn of Plenty, ever ancient, ever fresh, milk-white moonlight word-made-flesh.

O sovereign STAG, to you our lovelorn cries arise like arrows. Love immortally wounded, save us. We are banished, barren, and snared. Climb down to free us, lead us home to headwaters, crags, and columbines.

O SWALLOW, winter ends when you come carelessly capering from heaven and build your nest beneath our eaves. Come, bird from paradise; though you be small and powerless, you are the invincible PHOENIX.

O Divine EAGLE, come and hover over us, your brood, who pierced the only pinions that can bear us up from death and sin to sun and everlasting love.

O LION of Judah, King of courage, come to crush our blighted bones and hardened hearts and with one roar restore your stillborn whelps to everlasting life.

5

Don't Stop the Party

Celebrate the Full Twelve Days

Melanie McDonagh

Hilaire Belloc once wrote a magnificently dictatorial account of a proper Christmas as celebrated by his family. And you know when the whole thing actually started? At 5 PM on Christmas Eve. It was then, and not before, that Belloc brought in the Christmas tree from the garden, and the decoration of it took place before Midnight Mass that night. The same tree was then discarded on Twelfth Night, the feast of the Epiphany, and while the tree was up the Belloc party season was in full swing.

Of course he was right. His gist cannot be reiterated too often: the feast of Christmas kicks off on the vigil, on Christmas Eve, and carries on for a whole twelve days. That is the momentum of the feast. Instead of which, we now have the curious circumstances that Advent has been abolished and Christmas has been hideously elongated before it happens, yet truncated when it should be happening. That is to say, the whole period of waiting for Christmas has been overtaken by the celebration of it.

> The whole period of waiting for Christmas has been overtaken by the celebration of it.

You get the Christmas department of Harrod's up and running by October, and the office Christmas party season, including the option of Christmas lunch with the trimmings, starts from November. By the time we actually get to Christmas, we're collectively partied out, and after the family celebrations on the day itself, the whole thing concludes on St. Stephen's

Day, or Boxing Day, just when it should be getting into full swing. Granted, people resurface to party on New Year's Eve, but, by and large, the assumption is that on 1 January the diet and exercise regime starts, to get the New Year off on to a proper footing. In other words, people start their fast and abstinence with a good five days of Christmas left to go. And precisely because the retail side of Christmas starts so early, the shops are actually holding the sales by Christmas Eve. It's handy if you've left your present buying until the very last minute, but it does take away a bit from the atmosphere.

Boycott or Celebrate?

Actually, it was only when I went to Germany a few years ago that I realized that in Britain Advent had been displaced by a premature Christmas. I was sent to Nuremberg to write about the Christmas fair—decorations, crib figures, mulled wine, the works—but it dawned on me gradually that it wasn't a Christmas fair at all I was at; it was explicitly an Advent market, and it was Advent, not Christmas, that people mentioned in the cathedral, in the restaurant near the market, and in the shop selling spiced Advent cakes.

> By the time we get to Christmas, we're collectively partied out. After celebrating on the day itself, the whole thing concludes on December 26, just when it should be getting into full swing.

Granted, it would be a bit too austere, excessively Bellocian, to boycott Christmas parties on the grounds they were happening in Advent. Last year I toyed with the idea of not putting up my Christmas decorations till Christmas Eve, but decided against it because such a gesture would have been interpreted by my friends as sheer sloth or unusual decorative minimalism. No, we can't hold ourselves aloof from the party spirit prior to Christmas, but what we can do is celebrate like blazes once it's under way and not stop until after 6 January, when the Three Kings arrive.

Twelfth Night

It's crucial to celebrate the last day of Christmas, the Epiphany, in style. And thanks in part to that useful carol, "The Twelve Days of Christmas," and in part to William Shakespeare's *Twelfth Night,* it is a feast with a batsqueak of secular resonance. In Ireland the day used to be known as the Little Christmas, or Women's Christmas, when the women put their feet up, and went visiting, and didn't do any cooking, and the men looked after them. I fancy the idea myself. But the very least we can do is have a perfectly enormous party on the night.

And the *sine qua non* is the French custom of the Twelfth Night cake, puff pastry with almond cream inside and a bean, the finder of which turns into the King or Queen of the Night and can boss everyone else around. Personally, I think that this is also the occasion for party games, on the grounds that this was always known as the Feast of Fools, but that's just me. I was at a wedding on the vigil of Twelfth Night last year for which a little play about the Three Kings had been specially written. It was charming, in a proper medieval pantomime way.

There aren't that many ways to be attractively, assertively Christian just now, but one of them is to have really good parties after everyone else has stopped having them. People would actually rather like being invited to have a lark during the forgotten days of Christmas, after their own celebrations are just a memory. Having a good time is the kind of evangelization I can handle.

His way with men has been to take men's way,
And that's the glory and the scandal both…
O, not the thunders and the lifted gates
He chose, and not exotic retinue
To bring Him flaming through
  the breathless towns
…not this,
But briefest pausing in the pulse of life,
With all our old simplicities unmarred,
With no rejections of the flesh we bear
The hearts we love with and the pain
  we know.
He slept our sleep and with us
  dreamed our dreams.

John Lynch

I shall attend to my little errands of love
Early this year,
That the brief days before Christmas may be
Unhampered and clear
Of the fever of hurry. The breathless hurry
That I have known in the past
Shall not possess me; I shall be calm in my soul
And ready at last
For Christmas: "The Mass of the Christ,"
I shall kneel
And call out His name;
I shall take time to watch the beautiful light
Of a candle's flame;
I shall have leisure...

Grace Noll Crowell

Part 2

Winter

Peace
Be with you, winter,
Whose rage and
Tempest
Restore to nature
Her sleeping
Strength.

Kahlil Gibran

In the bleak mid-winter
Frosty wind made moan,
Earth stood hard as iron,
Water like a stone.
Christina Rosetti

"Winter" comes from the Germanic word *wintruz*. Solstice comes from two Latin words: *sol*, meaning "sun," and *sistere*, "to stand still."

As winter arrives and the days shorten in the Northern Hemisphere, some of us cope with the cold and darkness by scheduling parties. Others set aside extra time for silence, reflection, and gazing at the stars. My own odd interests lead me to reflect on the stars with Arabic names.

I once saw a planetarium program on the history of our fascination with stars and learned of the gnawing fear that gripped our ancestors at the winter solstice: how could they be sure the sun would return? Maybe the light would continue to dwindle, bringing cold, dark doom. Prayer and sacrifice were means for propitiating the angry sun.

We know different kinds of fear. Jesus came to free us from the crippling fear of a basically cruel or indifferent universe, the fear that without a loving God, dark spirits will snuff out the feeble glow of our own brief candles.

Jesus came, as Christina Rossetti wrote, "in the bleak mid-winter." He came as light, life, and fidelity. In response, we are moved by another kind of "fear," a holy fear that is really a humanizing awe, the first step toward wisdom. If we are awake and courageous enough to weather the darkness of a broken world and acknowledge our share in impeding the light, then the dark silent night of winter may become St. John of the Cross's "glad night," a "night more lovely than the dawn." Then we will be ready to receive the "logic of Love," whose smile like lightning sleeps in our paper flesh, waiting to explode and spread the fire of Christ to renew the face of the earth.

Enjoy winter's cold starry nights, walking on frozen lakes, reaching for the moon. And be careful not to fall through the ice like I did one winter—a chilling baptism I don't recommend.

—*David Denny*

Sonnet for the Winter Solstice
Robert Rose

Now ice spreads its hand on the windowpane
And wind shakes the rafters of this old place,
The fields lie fallow in the freezing rain
And the steepled hills bare their frozen face.
Now winter's cold ambush descends on us
And black seeds sleep under the flight of skies.
Darkness arrives; all is anonymous,
The sun has gone and the fading year dies.
So here we will wait while the candle burns
For that moment, as vast as tenderness,
When the first syllable of light returns
And covers the broad earth with a caress
Of visible air, so soft and so bright,
That the break of day will enfold the night.

Glad Tidings for Winter

the crunch of cold causes movement
toward the center of one's being
Janet Callewaert, O.S.M.

Winter is a time of clarity and simplicity. A time to begin, when
there is less importuning, less distraction of the senses. The branches
are bare and the far ridge visible…. Now the extreme cold brings
its true, appropriate gift: the narrowing down. Withdraw to one
room. Put on your reading glasses.
Josephine Johnson

Charm with your stainlessness these winter nights,
Skies, and be perfect!
Fly vivider in the fiery dark, you quiet meteors,
And disappear.
Thomas Merton

No one can walk in a road cut through pine woods without being
struck by the architectural appearance of the grove, especially in
winter when the bareness of the trees shows the low arch of the
Saxons. In the woods in a winter afternoon one will see as readily
the origin of the stained glass window…in the colors of the western
sky seen through the bare and crossing branches of the forest.
Ralph Waldo Emerson

God's fingerprints are everywhere. Nothing has ever been written
by theologians about God's beautiful presence that hasn't been
better traced in the crystal calligraphy of a frosty morning.
Daniel O'Leary

In the midst of winter, I finally learned that there was in me an
invincible summer.
Albert Camus

6

Stillness, Stars, and Motion

A Winter Reflection

David Denny

On the shortest day of the year, I hiked in freshly fallen snow up the rugged road that leads to St. John of the Cross Hermitage. The tiny wood frame hut hangs on a precipitous slope near the "rollrock highroad" of Willow Creek in Colorado's Sangre de Cristo Mountains. I arrived sweating from the ascent, but around 4:45 PM the sun set, the chill seeped through the thermopanes, and I lit a fire. I feel as if I'm hanging in the gondola of a hot air balloon when I go to John of the Cross. The slope to the south and west is so steep that I feel suspended as I gaze over the San Luis Valley and watch the scattered ranch lights flicker on in the gloaming. Venus hung in the west's afterglow, and a crescent moon followed her.

Scintilla and Selene

In a setting like this, sunset, Venus-set, and moonset are breathtaking events. In the silent stillness of that outpost, I was amazed at the sense of motion I felt as Venus passed through the silhouetted needles of a tall nearby spruce tree. This scintilla representing the goddess of love is never far from the all-consuming sun and, instead of stillness, I sensed her riding the wake of an irresistible presence.

An hour or so later, the silver sliver moon, Selene, slipped like a scimitar behind the San Juan Mountains, leaving the faintest afterglow and yielding the fathomless stage to Orion, who lumbered up from the east.

Star is one of my favorite words. I also love *stella*. Compostela, "field of stars," is a beautiful name. I also remember a movie character named Stella. She ran a saloon in *Silverado*! The place was called "Midnight Star." Stella was small, and she took a shine to a cowboy named Payton who became her bouncer. As he leaned against the bar one quiet afternoon, he asked her about her name. She got a wry, flirtatious twinkle in her eye and informed him that her name meant *star*, and it suited her because "Stars may be small, but they always shine at night!"

> Stella got a wry, flirtatious twinkle in her eye and told the cowboy that her name meant "Star" and suited her because "Stars may be small but they always shine at night!"

Stars and Arabs

To return to more celestial reflections, I love watching the constellations at this time of the year. The short days mean we spend a lot of time with the stars, and suspended in solitude above the edge of the San Luis Valley, I begin to wonder about their names and their stories. I know so little mythology. But it's a haunting feeling to stand under the canopy of hunters, soldiers, an eagle, a crow, two bears, seven sisters, a virgin and a lion. Looking at them I'm looking back in time, not at what is but at what was long, long ago. Stargazing also connects me with my Arabic interests. Some of the stars bear Arabic names:

Aldebaran ("the two followers"), Altair ("the flyer"), and Fomalhaut ("the fish's mouth").

I think of the Bedouins who navigate through deserts by the stars, and at this time of the year, the Magi come vividly to mind. G.K. Chesterton says that with the Magi's discovery of the star, God confirmed that although to some extent our destinies revolve around the stars, the deeper truth is that the stars revolve around the Christ-Child, the Logos. No matter how impossible it seems in a universe where we are less than dust and sometimes treated worse, we are not in the hands of Fate. Love is our destiny. As Dante put it, we are in the hands of the "love that moves the sun and the other stars."

> Some of the stars bear Arabic names: Altair ("the flyer"), Fomalhaut ("the fish's mouth") and Aldebaran ("the two followers").

Wandering Planets

This has also been a good time for planet-gazing. A friend once told me that the planets were ominous to our ancestors because their paths across the sky are irregular and very difficult to predict. *Planet* means "wanderer." I discovered that the word *flâneur* comes from the same root. A *flâneur* is a streetwalking wanderer, pickpocket or con artist. Yet the planets bear godly names. These gods of love, war, commerce, and agriculture are majestic, but also cruel, capricious or picaresque. The son of Mary doesn't appear that way to me. Again, in Chesterton's metaphor, it is a relief to know that Venus, Mars, Mercury, Saturn, and Jupiter revolve around the manger and the God in the straw. The powers they represent are great and their influence is difficult to predict in our lives, but in the end, I trust the Child.

Ice Walk

Reaching for the Moon

Tessa Bielecki

At eventide I walked through the snow up Moose Lake Road. The sunset was mauve and amethyst, shot with amber at the horizon, punctuated by bare black trees, the hooting of an owl, and ice music played by the run-off from the spruce bog rushing through the metal culvert under the road. As the darkness enveloped me, I made my way home with a waxing moon palely lighting the patches of ice in my path.

When the moon climbed higher and the Big Dipper turned upside down, spilling stars into the lake, I hiked across the ice through the channel, past the beaver dam, and into the second lake. I stopped in the middle before the island where the loons build their nests and traced my favorite star trek: from the top of Orion's right "shoulder" through the Seven Sisters and on to solitary Aldebaran. I became enamoured of that stunning red star when I first began to rise at 3 AM to go to chapel and met him every cloudless morning, directly in front of me on the path, glowing in all his ruby glory. "Are you one of God's sleepless eyes," asked Miguel de Unamuno in one of his poems, "forever awake, an eye scanning the darkness?"

I soon was seduced and stretched out flat on my back until I went numb with the cold, listening to the rumble of the ice freezing beneath me, and making love to the shimmering moon. On nights like these I suffer agony and ecstasy simultaneously. My heart swells with joy at the vision of so much glory and at the same time aches with longing for more intimate vital union with everything around me, behind me, before me, underneath me and over my head. No matter how passionately I pressed my eager body into the frozen lake or how vehemently I reached for the moon, I barely began to enjoy the union I longed for.

7

Icebreaker

Frost Flowers and Mother Earth

David Denny

I fell through the ice yesterday. The experience, coupled with a walk and skate on the lake this morning, also figuratively "broke the ice" for me. During a solitary week I'm usually invigorated by exciting ideas or projects. Not so this week. I'm supposed to edit an article—an easy job. But I haven't been able to. I think I can now: danger and movement help.

Psychedelicious Winter

Winter on a lake in Nova Scotia can be psychedelic. I have a lousy dictionary so I can't say what *delic* means. I'll make it up. *Psyche* is soul. *Delic* could mean "to blot out," which is one way to look at psychedelic drugs (deleterious). But pretend the *delic* means "delectable," "delicious." Winter here can be psychedelicious. Summer is visceral: sweat, seed, earth, birth, blood. Winter is sublime: glacial, contemplative, ethereal, aged, and wise. These poles occupy points on the seasonal spectrum, in a continuum. Today is the solstice. No wonder the psychedelicious pole prevails!

On my walk I saw lacy "frost flowers" (Tessa's term), which sprout from the iced lake surface on cold, calm nights.

When the sun came up, they caught the rays and mirrored them. I think I see white when I look at snow, but then what color is the gleam one of these petals casts? I heard them break under the force of the sun's rays. All across the tingling surface of the lake, the flowers burned. The night before, I was thinking that the winter sky magnifies the stars, not in size but in intensity. That's what these frost flowers look like: little stars with enough hibernally magnified light to rival the sun. These could be a comet's tail, settling like dust on the lake.

Celibacy and Sublimation

On my way home I saw small tornadoes of mist rising from the ice. As a student I was intrigued to learn about "sublimation" in chemistry class. Certain chemicals (I think iodine is one) can sublimate: they pass directly from crystal to gas without melting into liquid. Winter is sublime: the frost on the lake absorbs radiant energy from the sun, and without melting, it turns to mist. These mist-twisters spiraled up between tree shadows that stretched far out onto the lake.

> Summer is visceral: sweat, seed, earth, birth, blood. Winter is sublime: glacial, contemplative, ethereal, aged, and wise.

Maybe celibates need to sublimate until they reach a certain simplicity. I hope I will. We have to go from the "mass" level of erotic desire to the "pneumatic" or "energy" level of mystical eros without passing through the "normal" path of making a family. Maybe union with God is like "plasma," the fourth state of matter, which has properties of all levels and new properties that the other three never thought of. We'll see. Observing sublimation in nature helps me trust it is not unnatural.

Speaking of spirituality as including rather than excluding "profane" aspects of life, I think I was pondering the wonder of baptism before I fell through the ice. Funny. I was considering how Jesus doesn't destroy our humanity. He gathers it up and baptizes it, revealing that nothing is "profane," a word that means "outside the temple." So we're all in: bread and wine, flesh and blood, fire and ice.

> Mary probably didn't go stagnant. I need to fall in the lake to wake up and see with new eyes.

On my way home I wondered about Mary's passion. Unlike me, she probably didn't need jolts and probably didn't go stagnant. I need to fall in the lake to wake up, start over, and see with new eyes. John Lynch gives a hint of mounting passion in *A Woman Wrapped in Silence:*

> *The hours then that moved across her heart*
> *Were not the soft, obliterating fall*
> *Of moments sifting as a dust to blur*
> *The edges of the first impress of joy,*
> *But were reiterated stroke of deep*
> *Incising that would ever cut more sharp*
> *And clear, until the moment that would be*
> *His last at Golgotha...*

Mary broke through the ice when she accepted an angel's invitation. I imagine she grew long legs that sank deep into the abyss of the icy earth, into her child's Passion. I imagine her with long arms and fingers that touched the sun's fire, the Son who clothed her with the sun. She reminds me of Juan Ramon Jimenez's poem:

My feet, so deep in the earth.
My wings, so high in the heavens!
And so much pain in the heart torn between.

What's wrong with me? I'm not attracted to miracle workers or gods pretending to be human.

What's wrong with me? I am not attracted to miracle-workers or gods pretending to be human. I long for a *human* filled with God while remaining human. I have never warmed up to fertility goddesses either. But I need and love a *Mother of earth*, humble as humus, ripe with humanity. I recently found an example of Mary as *Mother Earth,* the earthy mystic, the humanized, baptized, fertility goddess. It comes from my "poetic theology" guru, St. Ephrem: "… for the sake of the flesh that is the Church incorruptible, this fleshly earth was blessed from the beginning, for Mary was the Mother Earth that brought the Church to birth."

It is winter proper; the cold weather, such as it is, has come to stay. I bloom indoors in the winter like a forced forsythia; I come in to go out. At night I read and write, and things I have never understood become clear. I reap the harvest of the rest of the year's planting.

Outside, everything has opened up. Winter clear-cuts and reseeds the easy way.... When the leaves fall the strip-tease is over; things stand mute and revealed. Everywhere skies extend, vistas deepen, walls become windows, doors open.... All that summer conceals, winter reveals.

Annie Dillard

Part 3
Christmas

The vagabond mother of Christ
and the vagabond men of wisdom
all in a barn on a winter night
and a baby there in swaddling clothes on hay
Why does this story never wear out?

Carl Sandburg

Joy to the world, the Lord has come,
Let earth receive her King...
And heaven and nature sing...
Traditional Carol

Christmas has meaning on so many levels, wrote

Caroline Kennedy in her anthology, *A Family Christmas*. The holy day and holiday intertwines the sacred with the secular.

When we prepare with stillness and simplicity during Advent, we feel ready to celebrate the full Twelve Days of Christmas, as people do all around the world with special customs, foods and drink. Bless each figure in your manger scene, meditate on The Word Made Flesh (Love *is* the "Logic"), the Unicorn Christ, and the Elemental Christ of earth, air, fire, and water. Enjoy our reflections on the books we love to read each year during the Christmas season, our favorite music and movies.

This season is not sentimental. Christ's cradle eventually becomes his cross. On December 26 we celebrate the feast of St. Stephen, the first martyr, who was stoned to death. On December 28 we remember King Herod's slaughter of the Holy Innocents. Both days commemorate sadly familiar tragedy, like today's headlines on CNN.

Commemorate the martyrdom of St. Thomas Becket on December 29 by inviting friends to read selections from T.S. Eliot's *Murder in the Cathedral* or view the 1964 film with Richard Burton and Peter O'Toole. *Joyeux Noel*, the story of the spontaneous Christmas truce during World War I, helps unite us to all those who celebrate Christmas in war-torn countries.

Such sobriety does not quell our joy. It is rather a sober intoxication with the paradox and beauty of a Baby who redeems the world that condemns him. The Word became flesh and loved it because he immersed himself in the whole catastrophe.

There's room for everyone beside the manger of the Infant Jesus, but we may discern a hierarchy, as Fr. Dave once wrote: "Ox and ass enter first! (This helps explain our several references to donkeys.) Then the childlike, such as Juan Diego, and the unpolished poor: shepherds, prostitutes and venal tax collectors." But the Tidings of Great Joy apply to everyone. "Born is the Son of Mary the Virgin," sings an old Scottish carol: "Behold his feet have reached the world... All hail! Let there be joy!"

—*Tessa Bielecki*

What good is it to us
For the Creator to give birth to his Son
If we do not also give birth to him
In our time and our culture?

Meister Eckhart

Glad Tidings for Christmas

Soft sound, a leaf turns
Oh sudden joy! At midnight
Clear, a Child is born.
Author Unknown

We follow the feet where all souls meet
At the inn at the end of the world.
G.K. Chesterton

O inexpressible mystery
and unheard of paradox;
the Invisible is seen;
the Intangible is touched;
the Eternal Word becomes
accessible to our speech;
the Timeless steps into time;
the Son of God becomes the Son of Man.
St. Gregory of Nyssa

Today all hatred dies
And tenderness is reborn.
The most misplaced heart
Now knows that someone cares.
Heaven is no longer alone.
Earth is no longer in darkness.
Juana de la Cruz

Remembering the stable where for once in our lives
Everything became a You and nothing was an It.
W.H. Auden

The world is large and complex, and sometimes there seems to be
no sacred ground. But in tent and palace...and under lighted trees
across the lands, the language of Christmas is universal.
Marcus Bach

A Christmas Carol

Directed by David Jones
www.warnervideo.com

Reflection by Tessa Bielecki

*W*ho can resist Charles Dickens' *A Christmas Carol* during the holiday season? This tale is not only a venerable cultural tradition but a spiritual meditation as well. Patrick Stewart makes a superbly nasty Ebenezer Scrooge in TNT's 1999 rendition of the classic. Stewart's genius is particularly evident in the scene of Scrooge's conversion on Christmas day. As the old man is reborn in the Spirit, he learns to lighten up and laugh, illustrating the depth of G.K. Chesterton's insight: "...the midst of the earth is a raging mirth."

Equally inspiring is the audio version produced by Simon and Schuster's Audio Division. Patrick Stewart thrilled audiences across America with his dazzling one-man stage production, creating all the voices himself from the Ghost of Jacob Marley to fragile Tiny Tim.

As one critic claimed: "A low tech audio Christmas card: no sound effects, no gimmicks, just one of the great voices of the contemporary classical stage creating as vivid a cast of characters as Dickens imagines. The Royal Shakespeare Company veteran...doesn't so much read the story as inhabit it with infectious delight." You, too, will be infected with the generous spirit of Christmas whether you listen alone or with your family.

> "God bless us every one!" prayed Tiny Tim,
> Crippled, and dwarfed of body, yet so tall
> Of soul, we tiptoe earth to look on him,
> High towering over all.
>
> *James Whitcomb Riley*

Blessing the Manger

(Say each prayer as you place the figure it names in the manger scene.)

Bless this manger, O Creator,
a sign of your love for us.

(Blessing Mary and Joseph)

Bless this household,
as you blessed Mary and Joseph.

(Blessing the angel)

Bless these Advent days;
guide the world with your
angel messengers.

(Blessing the shepherds)

Bless our daily work;
may it always point the way to you.

(Blessing the animals)

Bless all earthly humbleness;
fill the world with your presence.

(Blessing the Magi)

Bless all who seek you;
may they find you.

(Placing the Christ-Child)

God of all joy and peace,
hear the prayers we offer today
and each day,

Amen.

Christmas
Jan Pienkowski

New York: Knopf, 1984, 1991

Reflection by David Denny

Read this book before Christmas Midnight worship. Its twenty-four pages recount the Nativity in the words of Matthew and Luke in the King James Bible. But Pienkowski's illustrations are the best part of the experience. Each two-page spread includes a whimsical painting of a fairy-tale Central European village or countryside. Most of the color appears in the skies; the figures and foregrounds are black silhouettes. The scripture quotations begin with colorful initial capitals and are surrounded with gilt-edged drawings of plants and silhouettes of animals.

All the figures are lithe and expressive, even in their two-dimensionality. The angels, too, are lithe, like teenage dancers. The Annunciation takes place as Mary hangs out laundry. Bethlehem has onion-domed churches. Dogs howl, and the hat flies off a terrified shepherd's head as he falls away from his campfire at the sight of the angel directing him to the Christ-Child. The little family escapes Herod on a stormy night. In the end, the Child returns safely from Egypt. Ripe wheat, red poppies, and blue thistles decorate the account. We find the end of the rainbow in the penultimate illustration: not a pot of gold, but a little boy under a grape arbor. It seems too sweet until you notice what the little boy is offering to Joseph: his fist holds three nails. Pienkowski leaves us with one last silhouette: a child waxing "strong in spirit," perched on an oak branch.

These few pages infuse the old story with an infectious sense of childlike wonder, and the dark silhouettes add an undertone of pathos, reminding us that although the Light came into the world, we still live in the shadowlands.

8

Christmas Customs around the World

Entwining Sacred and Secular

Tessa Bielecki

One of the most beautiful Christmas customs comes from Ireland. On Christmas Eve, candles burn in every window of the house so that Mary and Joseph can find their way. The candles must shine all night and may only be snuffed out by someone named Mary. The door of the house is also left open as a sign of hospitality. As Irish poet Sigerson Clifford wrote from County Kerry:

> *Don't blow the tall white candle out*
> *But leave it burning bright,*
> *So that they'll know they're welcome here*
> *This holy Christmas night...*
> *Leave the door upon the latch,*
> *And set the fire to keep,*
> *And pray they'll rest with us tonight*
> *When all the world's asleep.*

Irish story-teller Eamon Kelly laments the fact that today instead of the old tallow candle there is "new garish, electric imitation lighting" in many of the windows. The "shy" quality of candlelight is different, he maintains: "the little lights winking and blinking through the dark until…the earth below seems a reflection of the starry heavens above."

The Irish celebrate Wren Day on December 26, the feast of St. Stephen. People disguise themselves in costumes and go from house to house and pub to pub, singing and raising money for charities. The wren holds place of honor among the birds of Ireland because he can fly highest—on the wings of the eagle! But the bird is also known for his treachery. According to legend, Stephen was hiding in a furze bush to escape his enemies, but a tiny wren betrayed his whereabouts. The wren also betrayed Irish soldiers fighting the Vikings by beating its wings on their shields. So the wren was once hunted and killed on St. Stephen's feast. Today the bird is spared and survives in the name of the day and in the traditional rhyme:

The wren, the wren, the king of all birds
On St. Stephen's Day was caught in the furze;
Although he is little, his honor is great,
So rise up, dear lady, and give us a treat.

December 26 is also known as "Boxing Day" in Ireland, England and other Commonwealth countries. How did the tradition originate? In medieval times, priests would empty the alms boxes in their churches on this day and distribute gifts to the poor. There is another explanation. Servants in the old manor houses were required to work on Christmas Day but given the following day off. As they prepared to leave and visit their families, their employers would present them with gift boxes.

Noel and *Nacimiento*

The French gave us our word *noel*, adapted from the Latin *natalis*, meaning "natal" or birthday. Noels were sung in Latin and French for centuries before the word found its way into English in the 1800s. France and French Canada have also given us *Le Gateau des Rois*. The Three Kings cake is baked with a bean inside. Whoever finds the bean when the cake is cut becomes King or Queen of Twelfth Night and gets to boss everyone around. The French use clay figures in their mangers instead of wood and often add ordinary people such as the butcher, the baker, and the priest.

After Midnight Mass in Spain, people parade through the streets singing *"Esta noche es Noche-Buena, y no es noche de dormir."* ("Tonight is the good night and not meant for sleeping.") Spanish children do not usually decorate Christmas trees or hang up their stockings. Their custom is called *nacimiento*: they hide slippers and shoes for Balthasar and the other Wise Men to fill with goodies on Epiphany. They leave out plums, walnuts, and cognac for each king, with water for the camels.

The Spanish celebrate Epiphany with an elaborate Three Kings parade, a float for each king, and traditional colors for their cloaks, beards, and hair. Gaspar, the King of Sheba, wears green. Melchior, the King of Arabia, wears gold. Balthazar, the King of Egypt, wears purple.

Germany and the Christmas Tree

The Germans not only gave us the immortal carol, *Stille Nacht* or "Silent Night," but *O Tannenbaum*, another popular Christmas song:

> *O Christmas tree, O Christmas tree,*
> *With faithful leaves unchanging.*
> *Not only green in summer's heat,*
> *But also winter's snow and sleet,*
> *O Christmas tree, O Christmas tree,*
> *With faithful leaves unchanging.*

No one really knows the origin of the Christmas tree. Evergreens were used for thousands of years in winter festivals in many cultures as a reminder that spring would indeed return.

The first documented use of an outdoor Christmas tree dates from 1510 in Riga, the capital of Latvia. The first German evidence is a picture dating from 1521. Was Martin Luther the first to decorate an indoor Christmas tree? The first indoor tree in England appeared in the 1830s. Prince Albert popularized the Christmas tree in 1841. Albert was Queen Victoria's German husband who set a tree up on a table in Windsor Castle for his royal family. A drawing of the tree was published in a London magazine and made its way to America. But German immigrants probably brought the tree to America even earlier.

The first decorations were candles and edibles: apples, pastries, and candies. The first tinsel was created in Germany from strips of beaten silver. According to Caroline Kennedy, the first electric Christmas tree lights, "eighty hand-blown red, white, and blue glass bulbs, festooned the 1882 tree of Edward Johnson, an executive in the Edison Illuminating Company."

The Yule Log

In earlier centuries before central heating, when we used enormous fireplaces, the yule log was an important custom in many countries. Could we not revive some of these customs today with smaller logs in our living room fireplaces?

On Christmas Eve the English used to bring a yule log into the house to burn. Each family member had to salute the log before it was lighted to assure the household good luck in the coming year. Bulgarian fathers brought in their logs on Christmas morning, while their families sprinkled them with corn to bring good health and bountiful crops. As the yule log was lit, the children struck it, making wishes as the sparks flew into the air.

When Yugoslavian men cut oak trees for their yule logs, the tree had to fall toward the east at sunrise. If any branches touched another tree, it was an omen of bad luck. On Christmas morning, a young neighborhood boy called the *polaznick* had to be the first to enter the house, throwing a handful of grain at each family member and asking a blessing. Concluding the ritual, he poured wine on the yule log and left a coin on one end to assure the family's good fortune.

The Three Kings in Syria

The Magi are also prominent in Syria's Christmas customs. On Christmas Eve, churches light bonfires in memory of the Magi who were cold from their journey. English poet T.S. Eliot called the Magi's journey "a cold coming" at "the worst time of the year" in "the very dead of winter."

According to a Syrian legend, one camel bearing the Three Wise Men was so young, he fell, exhausted by the journey. The Christ-Child blessed him with immortality. So the Syrian "Santa Claus" is the camel, who brings children gifts on New Year's Day. Instead of milk and cookies for Santa, the children set out wheat and a bowl of water for the camel. In the morning the good find presents, and the naughty find a black mark on their wrists, similar to the black lumps of coal American children sometimes find in their stockings.

St. Francis and the Manger Scene

The *precepio,* or manger, symbolizes Christmas in Italy and comes to us from St. Francis. In 1223, Francis created the first manger scene with real people, a real stable, a real ox and a real donkey. The Incarnation was a key element in his spirituality. He wanted to celebrate the feast in a way that would help people remember the Christ-Child born in Bethlehem poverty.

Italians set up their mangers as early as December 8, Feast of the Immaculate Conception, but don't put the baby Jesus in his crib until Christmas Eve. They often add everyday objects and people to their scenes, as the French do. The largest Christmas crib in the world, located in Naples, has 600 figures!

Another Italian gift to Christmas comes from St. Alphonsus Liguori. He wrote *Tu scendi dale stele,* "You came down from the stars," the most popular Christmas song in Italy, played on the streets during Advent.

> On the Feast of St. Lucy, a daughter of the family dresses in white with a crown of burning candles on her head.

The Cold North

Norwegians and Finns give special honor to animals and birds on Christmas, since they were the only ones present at the birth of Jesus. They give their farm animals extra fodder and leave out a sheaf of wheat for the birds to eat. Norwegians also light a candle every night from Christmas Eve until New Year's. Traditional tree decorations include small paper baskets shaped like hearts. Hans Christian Andersen, of fairy-tale fame, may have invented these in the 1860s.

In Sweden the Christmas season begins on December 13,

the feast of St. Lucy. A daughter of the family dresses in white with a bright red sash around her waist. As she moves through the house, waking the members of her family with coffee and saffron cakes, she wears an astonishing crown of fire: pine boughs with seven glowing candles.

Even farther north within the Arctic Circle, where the sun never rises in winter, the Inuit peoples of Greenland put illuminated stars in their windows. They decorate driftwood Christmas trees with heather unless they import evergreens from Denmark or Iceland. Favorite Christmas presents include sealskin mittens and polished walrus tusks. On Christmas Eve the men serve the women. "Merry Christmas" in Greenlandic or Inuit is "*Juullimi Ukiortaassamilu Pilluarit.*"

> A sheaf of grain in the corner signifies the family's Guardian Angel.

Poland and the Christmas Wafer

Polish people celebrate Christmas Eve with traditions that are both earthy and deeply spiritual. They place straw under the tablecloth in memory of the Child born in a stable and don't start their festivities until the first star appears in the sky.

Then they begin their age-old Vigil Feast, *wigilia* (pronounced vee-GHEE-lee-uh), with the breaking and sharing of the sacred Christmas wafer, the *opłatek*, from the Latin *oblatum* or "oblation." The *opłatek* is also a symbol of unity and peace on earth. Each person breaks off a piece and exchanges it with everyone else present, with blessings and good wishes.

A sheaf of grain in a corner of the house represents the family's Guardian Angel. An empty place may be set at the table for departed ancestors or for Christ himself, in hope that the unexpected Guest will come and bless the gathering. The Polish believe that "a guest in the home is Christ in the home." Poet Joyce Kilmer expressed the same hope when he wrote:

Unlock the door this evening
And let your gate swing wide,
Let all who ask for shelter
Come speedily inside.
What if your yard be narrow?
What if your house be small?
There is a Guest is coming
Will glorify it all.

Christmas in Warm Countries

In the warmth of the Philippines, palm leaves and colorful flowers replace the Christmas tree. On Christmas Day, children visit their godparents and older relatives, kissing their hands and receiving small gifts. Costa Ricans make their Christmas wreaths of cypress branches and red coffee berries. Their gift-bringer is *Niño Dios*, the Child God, Jesus, and their Midnight Mass is called *Misa de Gallo*, Mass of the Rooster, because they believe a rooster crowed the night Jesus was born. People in India decorate banana or mango trees; in New Zealand they decorate the *pohutakawa,* which has red flowers. In Nigeria, women sing and dance from house to house on Christmas afternoon. In the Congo, "Merry Christmas" is *"Mbotama Malamu."*

The Gift-Bringers

Who brings Christmas presents around the world? In Denmark it's the Christmas Man (*Julemanden*), in Chile the Christmas Old Man (*Viejito Pascuero*), in Hungary Old Man Winter (*Télapó*), in Bosnia Grandfather Frost (*Djeda Mraz*). Welsh children receive gifts from Chimney John, *Siôn Corn*, Afghan children from *Baba Chaghaloo*, and Hawaiians from *Kanakaloka*.

74

Las Posadas

An Hispanic Christmas Tradition

Bilingual Version by

Larry Torres

For nine nights before Christmas Eve, Hispanic communities all over the American Southwest reenact the story of Joseph's search for an inn where Mary could give birth to Jesus. Las Posadas *is celebrated as a folk opera. A procession moves from house to house in the neighborhood. Outside each home, the* posadistas *sing Joseph's verses as he begs for shelter. Those inside sing the part of the innkeeper who claims there's no room in the inn, so "Why not stay outside?"*

Farolitos, "small lanterns" in Spanish, often line the adobe walls and flat rooftops. These are small paper bags filled with dirt, with a yellow votive candle nestled inside each one. (Now they are often electric, more efficient, but with a less appealing glow.) Farolitos *are a modern offshoot of* luminarias, *"small bonfires" in Spanish, and safer in populated areas.*

Outside:

From a heavy journey,
We have come distressed,
Humbly we implore you,
For a place of rest.

Inside:

Who knocks at our portals,
With noise like thunder,
On this night inclement,
To disturb our slumber?

Outside:

Who will give us lodging,
Pilgrims both we be,
Tired from our journey
As you well can see?

Inside:

We've no vacant corner,
Where you two can hide,
But the fields are empty,
Why not stay outside?

Outside:

Great need is afflicting,
My dear wife divine,
We ask but a corner,
Where she may recline.

Inside:

Who disturbs the quiet,
Which by night we keep?
Get thee from our doorstep,
Don't disturb our sleep.

Outside:

The night marches onward,
For God's sake have pity,
Give the Queen of Heaven,
A room in your city.

Afuera:

De larga jornada,
Rendidos llegamos,
Y así imploramos,
Para descansar.

Adentro:

¿Quién a nuestras puertas,
En noche inclemente
Se acerca imprudente,
Para molestar?

Afuera:

¿Quién les da posada
A estos peregrinos,
Que vienen cansados,
De andar los caminos?

Adentro:

No hay rincón vacío,
Que puedan franquear
Vacío está el campo,
Y en él hospedad.

Afuera:

Necesidad grave,
A mi esposa aflige.
Un rincón les pido,
Donde se recline.

Adentro:

¿Quién es quién perturba,
De noche sosiego?
Márchense de aquí
No nos quite el sueño!

Afuera:

La noche avanza,
Por Dios condoléos,
Qué descanse un poco,
La Reina del Cielo.

Inside:
We'll no longer listen,
To foolish requests,
And the fields are vacant,
Make yourselves our guests.

Outside:
Joseph and his Mary,
Darling of his eyes,
At your door seek shelter,
From the winter skies.

Inside:
Welcome, lovely maiden,
Treasure of our coffer,
To you and your husband,
Our house now we offer.

Outside:
This is no small favor,
Which for us you do,
Heaven ever-watchful,
Will reward you too.

Inside:
Open doors and curtains,
Let the feast begin,
For the Queen of Heaven,
Comes to dwell within.

Adentro:
Ruegos importunes,
Ya no escucharemos,
Vacío está el campo,
Y en él recogedos.

Afuera:
Es José y María,
Su esposa amada,
Que a sus puertas vienen,
A pedir posada.

Adentro:
Entrad, bella Niña,
Tú y tu esposo,
Ésta es vuestra casa,
Que humilde ofrezco.

Afuera:
No tengáis en poco,
Esta caridad,
El cielo benigno,
Os compensará.

Adentro:
Abranse las puertas,
Rómpanse los velos,
Que viene a posar,
La Reina del Cielo.

Christmas in Calico

Jack Curtis

New York: Daybreak Books, 1998

Reflection by Tessa Bielecki

Christmas in Calico is an American homage in frontier literature to Charles Dickens' *A Christmas Carol*. Nine months pregnant, newly widowed, bank note due on the ranch, sick child, thieving neighbors: Rose Cameron's burden was almost too much to bear. But she'd promised her husband as he lay dying that she would hang on to the horse ranch at all costs for the sake of their children. Now she finds herself in the middle of a range war, and the only thing standing between her and total destitution are thirty-five turkeys that need to get to market before an impending winter storm.

But when young Tommy comes down with a mysterious fever, Rose has to abandon the turkeys to rush Tommy to the doctor in Calico. Once there, with no money for medicine or lodging, Rose walks from door to door, exhausted, worried and carrying her sick child, in search of shelter from the storm. Only the proprietors of an old stable-turned-diner in Shantytown take pity on Rose and offer her shelter, comfort and friendship.

Calico was rotting, inside and out. The bitterness of life on the range and the life-and-death struggle over water combined to create a tightness of spirit among the townspeople. Fear had the people of Calico in its grip. But a troubled stranger on a dark horse rode into their lives and with him came the miracle of change. One fresh voice, one new outlook, one brave soul was all it took to bring the spirit of Christmas to Calico.

9

Love is the Logic

The Word Became Flesh

David Denny

The Word was made flesh. This simple sentence still stuns me. It summarizes Christmas and proclaims the fulfillment of an ancient longing to see the Divine. The Latin version has a beautiful ring: *verbum caro factum est.* Each word highlights a human desire.

The hunger for meaning is the search for the *verbum.* The search for a Source that is both transcendent and immanent, tangible, even homely, is the yearning for *caro.* "Show us the light of your face, O Lord," the psalmist cries. And the impossible dream of fullness of life and triumph over injustice becomes realistic in *factum est.*

According to British writer G.K. Chesterton, we understand the Christmas story better when we notice who hears it first: the Magi, the shepherds, Herod, and, I would add, Mary.

The Magi

If we have a sense of wonder and curiosity, we are already amateur philosophers. We have questions about the basic structure and meaning of life, what ancient Greeks called the Logos, the Word. Our word *verb* comes from the Latin for *word*, but I like how it connotes action as well as speech in English. How does a word both say and *do* something?

> The Magi represent the tradition of Lao–Tse, Socrates, the Buddha, and anyone who searches the sky, the mind, and the heart for wisdom.

What is the grammar of silence? How do we creatures relate to the Mysterious One, the creative Source, Being itself? What is the pattern and end of history? Is there a coherent, transparent logos, logic, word, verb, or event that fits into the locked door of Mystery like a key and unlocks Truth? Is life a random accident or is there a principle at the core of all life, like the formula for calculating the area of a triangle, or the ratio between the circumference and the diameter of a circle? Is there a practice that will help us open up to the Real, the Principle, the Mystery?

In the Christmas story, the Magi represent the tradition of Confucius, Lao-tse, Socrates, Pythagoras, the Buddha, and anyone who searches the sky, the mind, and the heart for wisdom. As an amateur, I suspect the message they received is that Jesus' birth both increases and satisfies an ancient eros of the mind. A hinted law of life is revealed. The silence of Mystery breathes in an infant. The ratio of God-to-man lies in a manger. The Logos, the logic, is love. Wisdom takes flesh in a baby Jewish boy who took flesh from a very wise woman. Chesterton claimed that until Christmas no one would have associated an infant with the Infinite: "It is no more inevitable to connect God with an infant than to connect gravitation with a kitten." For me, Christmas is an epiphany of Wisdom. Strangely, the birth of a baby may give birth to wise visions that can help us broaden and deepen, just as Jesus "grew in wisdom and stature."

The Shepherds

The shepherds are not as interested in the Logos as they are in knowing and loving a God who will pitch a tent with them, speak to them in their own language, whom they can see and touch. "Primitive" peoples specify sacred places and times and rites where God dwells. Have we outgrown this primitive longing? When we become "civilized" and dismiss our primitive desires as folly and superstition, does the child in us die, locking us out of the Kingdom? My own intuition is that when the child is malnourished, our primitive nature rebels and we wrestle with addictions, compulsions, violence and depression.

If our childlike nature dies, we feel alienated from ourselves, each other, and God. The antidote to alienation is homecoming. We can't go back to Eden, so the Holy comes to our home, to our flesh. Heaven became as homely as a manger in a cave.

Homecomings remind me of the time when God took off his sandals and entered a house, and give me hope in a final homecoming, a heavenly banquet, the resurrection of the body. They affirm the shepherds' homely conviction that matter matters, that although the flesh veils, it also reveals; it is a pitiful and powerful epiphany.

Herod

Factum est. The main reason I love the Latin translation is the word *factum*. It is a fat word. It carries weight and has punch. When we use words like *became* or *was made*, we dilute the pithiness of *factum*. The Incarnation is a fact. "Heaven and earth may pass away, but my word will not pass away." The Word became flesh and Herod's flesh crawls. Why? Maybe he senses a new disobedience is born, and no power, terror nor anything created will corner or crush it.

> Christmas helps me trust that terror may be transfigured by someone who appeared in a starlit cradle.

The birth of Christ is the birth of a non-violent warrior. His weapon is powerless love. So Christians are militant about peacemaking. Jesus' spirit undermines power and subverts hatred, falsehood, and death. In *The Source,* James Michener describes how to destroy a castle by tunneling beneath it, stuffing the tunnel with dry wood, and setting fire to it. The heat in the tunnel spreads up the castle walls, weakens the mortar, cracks the stones, and the battlements fall. The child born in the cave was like that flame. His body, the underground community of the catacombs, fed that flame beneath Rome's walls, attempting to undermine an empire with love. We are still trying.

Spiritual communities end up being persecuted because their defense of the marginalized and innocent can threaten authorities, whether in Moscow, Soweto, Washington or in ourselves. Christ is innocent, but not innocuous. He is an inoculation. Sin is a tricky word. But when I think of it as disease, it gets less tricky. I think of power as one of sin's favorite homes. So an inoculation against sin meets powerful resistance. New Herods and Caesars slaughter innocents in Bethlehem, Jerusalem, Rome, Auschwitz, San Salvador, Baghdad or New York. Can a baby's birth inoculate us against despair? I hope so. That baby grew up to feel the full force of injustice. Christmas helps me trust that violence and terror may be transfigured by someone who appeared in a starlit cradle and later suffered the creative crucible of the cross. "Be of good cheer. I have conquered the world." I take that as a fact.

Mary

But the Christmas message is not only militant. It is matrimonial, too. St. John of the Cross uses both kinds of imagery in the *Spiritual Canticle:*

> *Our bed, a couch of roses,*
> *guarded by dens of lions with their young;*
> *our room which peace encloses*
> *her purple curtains swung; our wall,*
> *with a thousand gold escutcheons hung.*

Since the inclusion of the Song of Songs in the Jewish Testament, Jewish, Christian and Muslim mystics have used the image of bride and groom as a metaphor for union between the human and the Divine. St. John of the Cross was a sixteenth-century Spanish Christian Carmelite. His poetry reminds me of some Sufi poems. In his *Spiritual Canticle*, the bride, the faithful soul, has become the spouse of Christ after a long "engagement," learning to love and serve, pray and forgive. The bridal chamber is a place of rest and peace, and the purple curtains signify love.

> Homecomings remind me of the time God took off his sandals and entered a house. Matter matters.

But the dens of lions and the gold escutcheons are the virtues the soul has fought hard to win. John of the Cross continues: "When the soul possesses the perfect virtues, each of them is like a den of lions in which Christ, the Bridegroom, united with the soul in that virtue and in each of the others, dwells and assists like a strong lion. And the soul herself, united with him in these same virtues, is also like a strong lion, because she thereby receives the properties of God."

As for the escutcheons, or shields, "these virtues...have a defensive value, like strong shields, against the vices which were conquered through the practice of virtue. As a result, the bride's bed in flower is crowned with them as her reward, and protected by them as by a shield."

Manger and Marriage Bed

We have grave concerns about national security. But John of the Cross reminds me that in the deepest sense, my real security is in my relationship with Christ.

The only way I know to that security includes suffering, loss and a gradual deepening of humble love possessed "with fortitude." This is a good description of Mary, who was "full of grace" and is honored by many Christians as the Mother of God and the Bride of Christ, the New Adam. As the New Eve, she is our mother, too. Christians believe that by virtue of what we celebrate at Christmas, the Divine wedded human history. On the cross, Jesus consummated the marriage of divinity and humanity. I try to realize and celebrate this fact of facts through my ongoing conversion. I try to *respond,* which literally means to answer the promise, Christ's espousal, with my own promise to love my neighbor and my Creator.

Mary carried Jesus for nine months. The mystic Meister Eckhart said Christmas is meaningless unless we, too, give birth to Christ. Our pregnancy and labor last longer than nine months. St. John of the Cross says it is achieved "gradually and in stages ...at the soul's pace," that is, over a lifetime.

In our faith, time and eternity commingle. We can view the Nativity through the eyes of Easter, and recognize Christ as both baby and eternal bridegroom. The manger is the marriage bed and the mother is the bride. Not even the cross can break that bond: *factum est,* forever.

A Family Christmas
Selected and Introduced by Caroline Kennedy

New York: Hyperion, 2007

Reflection by Tessa Bielecki

"Christmas is a holiday of hope," writes Caroline Kennedy in her introduction to this colorfully illustrated family anthology. But "hope can bring disappointments" and "love can be painful," she continues. "And the powerful emotions of the holidays are not always easy to manage."

With this realism she gives us Christmas poetry, prose, sacred scripture, short stories, and beloved song lyrics from writers as varied as Charles Dickens, Martin Luther King, William Shakespeare, Garrison Keillor, e.e. cummings, Lawrence Ferlinghetti, Ogden Nash, Pearl S. Buck, St. Augustine, Mark Twain, John Lennon and Yoko Ono.

Henry Van Dyke sets the tone at the beginning of the volume: "Are you willing to believe that love is the strongest thing in the world—stronger than hate, stronger than evil, stronger than death.... Then you can keep Christmas. And if you keep it for a day, why not always?"

So many treasures here from the Kennedy family: an angel painting of Jackie's tucked into a ribbon on the front cover, Caroline's own wish list for Santa in 1962, and most touching of all, a letter her father wrote as president in October of 1961 to assure a young child that the Russians would not bomb the North Pole and keep Santa from making his rounds on Christmas Eve.

Kennedy reveals that her family's Christmas preparations "tended to the literary rather than the culinary," with the exception of "a few Christmas cookies." And her house was "a last bastion of the Victorian era, when a fresh orange was considered a special treat." She says that her mother was "certainly alone in her view that walnuts were appropriate stocking stuffers." (My own mother felt the same!)

I loved "The Computer's First Christmas Card" by Edwin Morgan, the "Santa Guide" for the Macy's department store Santas, vivid ethnic insights from Sandra Cisneros, César Vallejo, and Gwendolyn Brooks ("Dreams of a Black Christmas"). The book includes particularly moving stories from Truman Capote about "fruitcake weather" and Harriet A. Jacobs's "Incidents in the Life of a Slave Girl," as well as classic favorites such as O. Henry's "Gift of the Magi" and Francis P. Church's "Yes, Virginia, there is a Santa Claus."

> Are you willing to believe that love is the strongest thing in the world—stronger than hate, stronger than evil, stronger than death.... Then you can keep Christmas.

We learn the history of celebrating Christmas from the Puritans' Massachusetts ban in 1659, through the 1820s when America began to invent the celebration we recognize today (Christmas was not declared a holiday in most states until after the Civil War), to New York State's founding of the St. Nicholas Society, transferring the holiday from the streets, where public drunkenness, licentious sex, and gambling prevailed, to the home, with children at the center. Clement Clarke Moore, who wrote "A Visit from St. Nicholas" in 1822, was a founder of the St. Nicholas Society.

"Rooted in the nativity and the teachings of Jesus," Kennedy concludes, "the desire for peace and the obligation to share one's blessings with those less fortunate have always been integral parts of Christmas."

10

The Unicorn Christ

A Unique Vision of Christmas

Tessa Bielecki

The legend of the unicorn teaches us something about the meaning of Christmas. Take a look at *The Unicorn Tapestries* published by the Metropolitan Museum of Art in New York City. The book is a series of lavish photographs and essays on seven elegant unicorn tapestries woven around 1500, the late Middle Ages, and now on permanent exhibition in an art gallery known as The Cloisters outside of New York City. *The Unicorn and Other Poems (1935-1955)* by Anne Morrow Lindbergh is a great accompaniment.

Another aid is Peter Beagle's *The Last Unicorn*, an odd and evocative little novel. The author combines comedy and pathos, terror and tenderness, paradox and wit in passages where the prose frequently bursts into poetry and song. And through Beagle's literary fantasy, we discover Christ in brand new, refreshing ways; we fall in love with him all over again; and we come to an enlivened understanding of Christmas.

The Last Unicorn

The unicorn in this novel is female, although most unicorns are male. But don't be distracted by the gender, because the unicorn, male or female, is unmistakably the Christ. Like Christ, the unicorn is eternal; as John's Gospel tells us, "with God in the beginning," and with "a light that shines in the dark, a light that darkness cannot overpower."

Christ comes down from heaven to redeem us from slavery, as we read in the letter to the Hebrews on Christmas Day. So the unicorn comes out of her secluded forest to free her people from the king whose wickedness is embodied in the Red Bull, a ferocious beast who has enslaved not only the unicorn but the entire countryside. Like Christ, to fulfill her divine destiny, the unicorn takes on human flesh and becomes mortal, "full of tears and hunger and the fear of death."

On her mission she is accompanied by a magician named Schmendrick, "a kind of upside-down Merlin" and a good model of the contemplative. Unlike the non-contemplative people in the world who are "bored with bliss, satiated with sensation, and jaded with jejune joys" (especially at Christmastime), the magician sees the world as "forever fluid, infinitely mutable and eternally new." The secret of this master wizard is the secret of every true contemplative: seeing and listening. As Schmendrick says, all the rest is merely technique.

Schmendrick and the unicorn are joined by Molly Grue, who is not exactly your virgin maiden! Ribald Molly has just entered middle age. She has been living in the woods for twenty years with the captain of an outlaw band and embodies every good womanly trait: she develops a special affection for everyone and anyone she feeds.

Together this unlikely group must trust the advice of a talking crook-ear cat, outwit a talking skull, and escape from a witch who weeps grains of sand, Mommy Fortuna, who runs a midnight carnival featuring "creatures of the night brought to light." Their archenemy is appropriately named Haggard, a king who lives in a dark, cold, lifeless castle and forbids everything "from lights to lutes, from fires to fairs and singing to sinning; from books and beer and talk of spring to games you play with bits of string."

Because the unicorn is Christ and it is through Christ that "all things come to be," as John's Gospel tells us, the eyes of the unicorn are "full of green leaves, crowded with trees and streams and smaller animals." She is wild and sea-white, "the colour of snow falling on a moonlit night." Her mane is "soft as dandelion fluff and as fine as cirrus." She possesses the "oldest, wildest grace that horses have never had, that deer have only in a shy, thin imitation and goats in dancing mockery."

Peter Beagle says the unicorn's luminous horn "shone and shivered with its own seashell light even in deepest midnight." Anne Morrow Lindbergh calls the horn a bright fountain "spurting to light of early morn," a white lily springing from the earth below, a majestic comet bursting from the animal's tranquil brow. If we were to interpret the letter to the Hebrews a little loosely through the magic of Christmas, we might call the unicorn's horn the "radiant light of God's glory." The horn glows in the dark to light the way; it kills dragons and knocks down ripe chestnuts for bear cubs. And like the cross of Christ it symbolizes, it is proof against death. Whomever the unicorn touches with her horn is resurrected from the dead.

Judeo-Christian Origins

This poetic imagery holds a very orthodox place in our Judeo-Christian history. Hebrew scholars living in Alexandria in the third and second centuries before Christ translated the Jewish Testament from Hebrew into a Greek version called the *Septuagint* because there were seventy-two scholars and they did the work in seventy-two days. These men put the unicorn in the biblical books of Numbers, Deuteronomy, Job and the Psalms. Like the original books of the Jewish Testament, this translation was considered divinely inspired, so it appeared obvious that the unicorn was authenticated by God. When St. Jerome translated his Jewish Testament, he turned the unicorn into a rhinoceros! Modern scripture scholars say the word the Alexandrian scholars translated as unicorn should be *wild ox.* What a pity that most contemporary versions say wild ox! They may be more linguistically and zoologically correct, but they miss the mytho-poeic point. The point is that the image of the unicorn has persisted, virtually unchanged, for over 2500 years.

Why? Because we feel an enduring need for such a symbol.

In another section of the letter to the Hebrews, we read: "At various times in the past and in various ways, God spoke to our ancestors." It seems that God spoke to our ancestors at various times throughout the ages through the symbolism of the unicorn, which he deeply imbedded in our collective unconscious, as part of the revelation of Jesus. Many early Christian mystics

> Wherever the unicorn passes, spring comes, everything shut up tight opens, and the silent rejoicing of the flowers is so loud that it keeps everyone awake.

and philosophers agree: Tertullian, St. Ambrose, Hugh of St. Victor, St. Albert the Great, St. John Chrysostom, and St. Basil, who developed the symbolism at length and calls Christ the "son of unicorns" because "the unicorn is irresistible in might and unsubjected to man." Two hundred years after the birth of Christ, the Christian community adopted the unicorn, not merely as a remarkable animal described by pagan writers and endorsed by the Bible, but as a symbol of Christ, the spiritual unicorn. As the unicorn surrendered his fierceness and became tame by means of a virgin maiden, so Christ surrendered his divinity and became man through the Virgin Mary. The unicorn is the ultimate image of purity. He is vulnerable precisely because he is pure. He cannot be taken and defeated by strength but only won by purity.

The Unicorn in Captivity

The Gospel for Christmas morning is not from Matthew, Mark or Luke, which tell the story of the birth of the baby Jesus. The Christmas morning Gospel is from John, the more theological Gospel, which interprets the *meaning* behind the birth of the baby. John is a perfect Gospel for a unicorn Christmas because it's so mysterious, mythical, and mystical.

Anne Morrow Lindbergh's poem, "The Unicorn in Captivity," is a perfect complement to St. John. Since you may not know the tapestry which inspired the poetry, let me describe the weaving. The unicorn is captured and enclosed in a corral, a fence of scarlet railing. He has a jeweled collar around his neck, a symbol of his taming, and he is tied by a thin gold chain to a pomegranate tree. This scene is usually considered a symbol of the Resurrection, but I also find it an appropriate image of the Incarnation.

The corral is the cradle, and the cradle is the flesh. When God became human in Jesus, he was cradled in human flesh, tied to the earth, captured by humanity as a prisoner of love. The refrain which Lindbergh uses over and over in her poem is the freedom of the unicorn in captivity, the unicorn, held captive in his human flesh out of love for enfleshed humanity. Christ, the spiritual unicorn, is free because he chooses to be captivated by us, his bride, the earth, all of humanity.

Pomegranate Vitality

The pomegranate tree is an exquisite symbol of the Church, the Bride of Christ. Under the red rind of the pomegranate, a very exotic fruit, you find a multitude of seeds. As the pomegranate has many seeds within one rind, so the Church is many peoples united in Christ. And Christ, the unicorn, is tied to his pomegranate tree, his Church, his Mystical Body forever, in the fidelity of perfect love and compassion.

The pomegranate is also a symbol of fertility. Christmas is about fertility, fecundity, fruitfulness. Why did Christ come? He tells us plainly later on in St. John's Gospel: "I have come that you may have life and have it more abundantly!" Peter Beagle's novel also makes this clear. Wherever the unicorn passes, new life erupts. The "rampaging greenness" of spring comes to a land cursed by winter for fifty years, everything made naked and bare by the cold is clothed in glory, everything shut up tight opens, and the silent rejoicing of the flowers is so loud that it keeps everyone awake.

"Unicorns are for beginnings," says Schmendrick the magician: "for innocence and purity and newness." When Prince Lir, the young knight-errant, sees the unicorn for the first time, he realizes that he has been a dead man, only now brought back to life. The unicorn looks as though she had just been born that morning. And she was.

> Unicorns are for beginnings, for innocence and purity and newness.

Hungry for Unicorns

In the first chapter of *The Last Unicorn,* one hunter asks another, "Would you call this age a good one for unicorns?" That's the question we have to ask ourselves at Christmas: Is this a good age for unicorns? When I was in New York City recently I went to an arts and crafts exhibit in Central Park. In every single booth I found a unicorn fashioned from every possible raw material: metal, paint, stained glass, wax, and wood. I was stunned to find the streets of the city filled with unicorns: shopping bags, books, posters, greeting cards, labels for alfalfa sprouts. Then I read about the "Unicorn Hunters," a world-wide society of writers, artists, and others who believe that "each of us is born with a unicorn to seek."

Our age may not be a good one for unicorns, but it's an age *hungry* for unicorns because we're hungry for the Divine, even though we may not know it. The unicorn is real because Christ is real and the unicorn is embodied in him. The unicorn Christ is an answer for every age. So this year when your friends wish you a Merry Christmas, wish them back a Unicorn Christmas, a Christmas, a season, a lifetime full of divinity.

The Donkey's Dream

Barbara Helen Berger

Philomel Books,
Putnam and Grosset, 1985

Reflection by Tessa Bielecki

"Slowly they came...a mere donkey carrying the hope of the world." This verse from an old Christmas card sums up the donkey's importance. Children's Christmas books often make this clear, especially *The Donkey's Dream* by Barbara Helen Berger, who also did the lovely illustrations. *The New York Times* compared her "jewel-like pictures" to an illuminated manuscript.

As Berger begins to weave her story, a small gray donkey is walking along on Christmas Eve, as usual, with a load on his back. In the starlight, the donkey begins to dream. He is carrying a city with gates and towers and temple domes. He is carrying a ship that rocks like a cradle and shines like the moon. He is carrying a fountain whose splashing waters make a garden spring up in the desert sand. He is carrying a rose, "soft as a mother's touch and sweet as the sleep of a baby." He is carrying "a lady full of heaven."

When the donkey finally stops for the night, he is tired, left alone outside with sore legs and an aching back, drinking from a watering trough lit up by a single star. Once the baby's cry rings out, "the man" brings the donkey into the cave, and "the lady's" tender response to the beast of burden warms our hearts as it does the donkey's heart.

As one reviewer put it, this story is "simple enough for young listeners to understand yet full of complexities for older children and adults to ponder." Berger's symbols and images are among those complexities. Like Phyllis McGinley in her

Wreath of Christmas Legends, Berger draws from the rich medieval era, rooted in Sacred Scripture, when Mary was called a "spiritual vessel," "Rosa Mystica," "ark and ship and breeze and haven, moon and lamp and coming home."

Let Berger's story and "soft, evocative artwork" bring you closer to "home" this Christmas season by filling you with the grandeur of the Nativity story. As English author G.K. Chesterton wrote, "in the place where he was homeless," all of us are "at home." And the donkey carries us there.

The Donkey's First Christmas

Kimberley Parr

Bath, UK: Paragon, 1998

Reflection by Tessa Bielecki

Children's books can make deep as well as delightful meditations for adults at Christmas when we celebrate the birth of the child in us along with the Christ-Child. Kimberly Parr was only eleven when she wrote *The Donkey's First Christmas,* winsomely illustrated by Emma Dodd.

The old cow in the stable is very upset about the crowds that keep pouring in: the tiny family, the shepherds and sheep, the Three Kings, and all those singing angels! "They're *not* all coming in here, are they?" she complains repeatedly, not unlike ourselves.

What a night! The donkey can't get any sleep either with all these visitors. Then he begins to wonder: Could there be something extraordinary about the newborn baby lying in the manger? Finally he understands and proudly boasts: "The first Christmas? Let me tell you about it. I was there!" A donkey's perspective is always inspiring.

11

Mary: Mother and Lover

The Manger and the Cross

Tessa Bielecki

My last Advent alternated between the anticipatory joy of the pregnant Virgin and the anguish of a world starved for a Savior. The first week I spent steeped in silence, the stillness of a pregnant Mary, waiting for her child to be born, the light to dawn, the earth (the womb) to open and bud forth the Messiah.

The next two weeks I felt inside my soul all the worry, weariness, and weakness of the broken world. I was intimately immersed in the world's sorrow, fear, anxiety, and loneliness, holding within my embrace weeping men, women, and children.

Both dimensions are characteristic of Advent and Christmas, too. Some vivid images help me plumb the depths of this mystery. The first is a crucifix with corpus made of simple black papier-maché and cross fashioned out of rough-hewn wood. Turned one way, the body of Christ rests in a cradle; turned another, the body writhes on the cross.

The second image is similar, only now the swaddling bands warming the baby become the shroud wrapping a cold dead adult. This drawing is all the more poignant because it was created by a suicidal guest who casually left it behind in a pile of papers to be discarded after his retreat. I rescued it and have prayed more vehemently for him ever since. (He disappeared from our lives.)

The third image comes from an article on sexuality entitled "Pure Passion," published by *Sojourners* magazine decades ago. You need to look at it twice and with two kinds of eyes: the eyes of the lover and the eyes of the mother. Look first, and you see the lover holding her beloved on her breast, enclosing him in the circle of her arms. Look again, and you see the mother carrying her baby in the womb, enclosing him in the circle of her belly. The mother and the lover are one. The baby in the womb is one with the grown-up lover on the breast, before or after his terrifying crucifixion. Mary the Mother, Mary the Lover; Jesus her Baby, Jesus her Beloved.

Musically this is expressed in my sister Connie's magnificent rendition of the traditional folk song, "Virgin Mary Had One Son," sung in tandem with "Weeping Mary Standing at the Tomb," the same tune with new lyrics written by Fr. Dave Denny especially for Connie. In the first song, Connie is Mary the Mother, joyously crooning for her newborn baby. In the second song, Connie is Mary the Lover, keening for her now-dead Beloved.

Arms Too Short to Box with God

This drama unfolds with similar splendor in a black Gospel musical called *Arms Too Short to Box with God* which I saw in New York in 1977. Imagine the scene: It's the day we now call Holy Thursday. The Scribes and Pharisees have made up their minds to get rid of Jesus. Judas has made his dirty deal and agreed to betray Jesus for thirty pieces of silver. Mary the Mother, Mary the Lover, like any good woman, intuits that "Something's wrong in Jerusalem." She "can't dismiss a nagging feeling." In this version of the Gospel, Mary the Mother is a large woman who can really belt out a song. She begins, "My son, precious one, where are you tonight? I wonder…"

At the same time, Mary the Lover, in the person of Mary Magdalene, a young, slender girl, is exquisitely dancing out her own agonizing apprehension. Though Mary the Mother and Mary the Lover, the Magdalene, are two persons in the musical, they really are one person.

Mary the Mother is massive, standing solemnly like a rock, with great strength and dignity. Mary the Lover dances with energy and eros in almost a frenzy. In the background, the women of Jerusalem sing like a Greek chorus of wailing women. They call out, "Mary!" And of course they mean both sides of the same person. "Mary, what's troubling you? Something's got you worried. You got a lot on your mind."

Mary Mama sings on: "When you were a boy, I could hold you and protect you." Then comes a killer of a line sung by mothers everywhere throughout the ages: "But when a boy becomes a man, what's a mother to do?" And then she cries out, "My Lord, precious Lord!" And back to "Where's that boy tonight, I wonder…"

"My son, precious one," sings Mary the Mother. "My Lord, precious Lord," sings Mary the Lover. The newborn babe, the grown-up man. The cradle and the cross. All carried in a woman's womb, a woman's arms, a woman's heart.

Every one of us, male or female, is this archetypal woman, carrying the same motherly-loverly burden. As Mary the Mother, we cradle the baby Christ, the fragile and vulnerable world, depending on us for nurturing and protection. As Mary the Lover, we cradle the crucified Christ, the suffering and broken world, with "pure passion," compassion, and love.

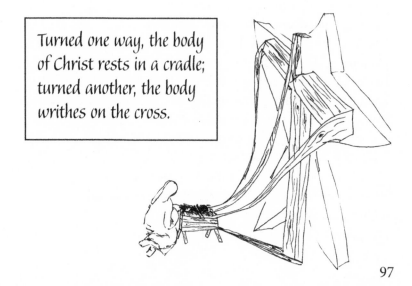

Turned one way, the body of Christ rests in a cradle; turned another, the body writhes on the cross.

Merriment...

Be merry, be merry,
I pray you every one!...
Now Mary for thy Sonnes sake
Save them all that mirthe make
And longest holdy on! Be merry!

Medieval English Carol

Heap on more wood!—the wind is chill;
But let it whistle as it will,
We'll keep our Christmas merry still.
Each age has deem'd the new-born year
The fittest time for festal cheer:...
Then open'd wide the Baron's hall
To vassal, tenant, serf, and all.
Then came the merry maskers in,
And carols roar'd with blithesome din;
If unmelodious was the song,
It was a hearty note, and strong.
'Twas Christmas broach'd the mightiest ale;
'Twas Christmas told the merriest tale;
A Christmas gambol oft could cheer
The poor man's heart through half the year.

Sir Walter Scott

This time of year is spent in good cheer,
And neighbors together do meet,
To sit by the fire, with friendly desire,
Each other in love to greet.
Old grudges forgot are put in the pot,
All sorrows aside they lay;
The old and the young doth carol this song,
To drive the cold winter away.
When Christmastide comes in like a bride,
With holly and ivy clad,
Twelve days in the year much mirth and good cheer
In every household is had.

Eighteenth-century English Carol

...In a Warring World

The wise guys tell me
that Christmas is Kid stuff...
Maybe they've got something there—
Two thousand years ago
three wise guys chased a star
across a continent to bring
frankincense and myrrh to a Kid
born in a manger
with an idea in his head...
And as the bombs crash
all over the world today
the real wise guys know
that we've all
got to go chasing stars again
in the hope
that we can get back
some of that Kid Stuff
born two thousand years ago.

Frank Horne

O Mother of God,
be hands that are rocking the world
to a kind rhythm of love:
that the incoherence of war
and the chaos of unrest
be soothed to a lullaby;
and the sorrowful world,
in your hands, becomes
the cradle of God.

Caryll Houselander

Baby Jesus was very small but his grown-up words could have a big impact upon our worried world.

Wanetta Rodney, Grade 4

The helpless newborn child in a lowly cave has come to heal life's wounds. In Christ we can recognize the face of every little child who is born, of whatever race or nation: the little Palestinian and the little Israeli; the little American and the little Afghan; the child of the Hutu and the child of the Tutsi... whoever the child is, to Christ each one is special.

Pope John Paul II

Here, in the midst of war... here amid all these tumults, we have tonight the peace of the spirit in each cottage home and in every generous heart. Therefore we may cast aside, for this night at least, the cares and dangers which beset us and make for the children an evening of happiness in a world storm. Here then for one night only, each home throughout the world should be a brightly lighted island of happiness and peace. Let the children have their night of fun and laughter, let the gifts of Father Christmas delight their play. Let us grown-ups share to the full in their unstinted pleasures before we turn again to the stern tasks and formidable years that lie before us, resolved that by our sacrifice and daring these same children shall not be robbed of their inheritance or denied their right to live in a free and decent world.

Winston Churchill at the White House, 1942

Joyeux Noel

Written and Directed by
Christian Carion
www.sonypictures.com

Reflection by David Denny

Joyeux Noel is not a "merry" Christmas film. Set during the First World War, it tells the true story of how traumatized German, French, and Scottish soldiers celebrated Christmas in 1914.

A solo piano accompanies the opening scenes: period snapshots of flowing rivers, family portraits, domestic security, and grammar school. That's where the trouble begins, as students recite "patriotic" racist poems.

A devout Scottish boy leaves his parish, to his priest's horror and his brother's delight. In an opera house, after an angelic *Ave Maria*, a German officer interrupts to announce the war's outbreak. And a young French officer, exhausted by life in the trenches, vomits as he suits up to command his troops. Then he strides into the trenches to lead a doomed bayonet charge.

In an age of drone warfare, we may forget how small a battlefield can be. Enemies are in shouting distance across a field strewn with frozen corpses. One French soldier watches a nearby farm at night, recalling that his own home is only an hour away, a world away, in German territory.

We see the chasm between the war planners in their world of art, music, and feasting, and life in the trenches. Although the soldiers respect their immediate commanders, their disdain for distant superiors runs darkly through the trenches and in the end turns back on them with chilling vengeance.

But now it is Christmas Eve. Scots are drinking and the bagpipes come out. German soldiers deck Christmas trees with candles. Scots and French are shocked to see these illuminated *tannenbaums* appear above the trenches' edge.

101

What happens next is for you to find out, and it's worth it. Just as it may be difficult to imagine how small a battlefield can be, we may also have trouble imagining that opponents may share a common faith. Can that faith reconcile enemies? Or will it serve as fuel for nationalist, racist sentiment? And if both, then which will prevail? In this tale, prince and prelate choose the latter. A soldier's "reconciliation" is a superior's "treason."

The movie offers portraits of PTSD before we had a name for it. Its bleakness reminds me of World War I veteran Wilfred Owen's "Dulce et Decorum Est," a poem that has haunted me for decades. (The title is from the famous sentence in the *Odes* of Horace: *Dulce et decorum est pro patria mori,* "It is sweet and fitting to die for one's county.") The sparks of hope remind me of Romanian writer Petru Dumitriu's conviction that the weight of evil in our world cannot be overcome by any greater weight, but it may be transfigured by seemingly weak and humble opponents: prayer and beauty.

We were in the trenches, and the Germans began to make merry on Christmas Eve, shouting at us to come out and meet them.... [We] met halfway, and there ensued the giving of cigarettes and receiving of cigars, and [we arranged]...a 48 hours' armistice.... Christmas Day was very misty and out came those Germans to wish us "A Happy Day."...So there you are; all this talk of hate, all this fury at each other that has raged since the beginning of the war, quelled and stayed by the magic of Christmas. Indeed, one German said, "But you are of the same religion as me, and to-day is the Day of Peace." It is really a great triumph for the Church. It is a great hope for future peace when two great nations, hating each other as foes have seldom hated, one side vowing eternal hate and vengeance and setting their venom to music, should on Christmas Day, and for all that the word implies, lay down their arms, exchange smokes, and wish each other happiness!

Letter written on December 28, 1914 to the London Times *from a Highland Regiment officer at the front.*

12

The Elemental Christ

Heart of the Cosmos

David Denny

Advent is a good season for reading. While waiting for the winter solstice and Christmas, I revisit the Gospels of Mark and John. The books differ, but both depict Jesus as prophet, lover and savior, and give hints of his intimacy with nature: earth, air, water and fire. During Advent I also read poetry and fiction through the lens of this "cosmic" Christ.

The Jesus of Mark moves with startling God-speed, arriving full-grown and rushing like a comet to Calvary. But John's Christ seems to process calmly from one miracle to the next with regal yet humble strength. After all, John says Christ is the Word who has always been here and always will be. I appreciate the contrast between these visions: the stark time-bound drama of Mark and John's quiet, awed confidence in the embodied eternal Word, Way, Truth, Light and Life of the world.

Mark does not begin with the pageantry of the Nativity. He goes straight to John the Baptist, whose message seems almost fanatic: time is running out; we need to change *now*. On the one hand I roll my eyes, imagining John as a world-hating delusional doomsday forecaster. On the other hand, I think about how many lives and worlds have already run out through poverty, war, terror, and greed, and I picture him as a sage who knows every life is short, our world is always ending, and it is always urgent to respond wisely.

> We meet the leonine and aquiline Christ: Son of the earth and soaring Lord of the sky.

"Let's Roll!"

In the ninth verse, Jesus appears as a grown man, not a baby: "In those days Jesus came from Nazareth of Galilee and was baptized by John in the Jordan." He arrives alone, and after the baptism, "the Spirit immediately drove him out into the wilderness." In the fourteenth verse, the Baptist is arrested and Jesus appears in public "preaching the gospel of God." I confess it reminds me of the old "Highway Patrol" episodes I used to watch on TV: Broderick Crawford gets a phone call, takes the address, slams down the phone, barks "Let's roll!" and in the next scene his boxy black-and-white patrol car careens around a corner, tires screeching, siren blaring. Mark does not waste words or time: Christ hurries to the scene of the crime.

On page two, Jesus surprises the people of Capernaum when they hear him in their synagogue. I get the impression they were used to platitudes and moralism, but Jesus sounded like someone who had passed through fire and would do it again for their sakes. By page three, he bristles at religious leaders who complain that he heals people on the wrong day of the week. By page four, Jesus' friends and some scribes say he is crazy. On the same page, demons claim he is divine. "You are the Christ," Peter proclaims on page ten, but this title had no official definition. We are slower than demons to arrive at certain conclusions.

Jesus keeps moving: Bethsaida, Caesarea Philippi, up the mountain, through Galilee, into Capernaum, to Judea and beyond the Jordan in two pages. "And they were on the road, going up to Jerusalem, and Jesus walking ahead of them." The book covers three years, and almost half of it covers one week. But the halt to physical movement during the final week intensifies the inner movement, the Passover from a brief life through a torturous death and impossible Resurrection. Not only does Mark omit the birth of Jesus; the earliest version omits the Resurrection, too. I wonder if it was like the Hebrew name for God: too unprecedented, sacred, beautiful and unimaginable to be written or spoken aloud.

Whereas Mark strikes me with Christ's swift stark trajectory, John welcomes me into the mystical presence and tenderness of the divine Shepherd. In the oldest manuscripts of Mark, the final words describe the experience of three women who come to Jesus' tomb after his death: "They departed and fled from the tomb, for trembling and fear had seized them; and they said nothing to anyone, for they were afraid." Such fearful unknowing speaks to soul-grinding traumas suffered in the Holocaust or portrayed in fictional characters like Sophie in William Styron's *Sophie's Choice*: crucifixion without resurrection, the death of God. When faced with that abyss, I find hope in the glorious Christ of John's gospel.

Lion and Eagle

Christ is a victim; Christians believe he is also a priest. He is a persecuted prophet; he is also the vanquisher of fear, hatred, and death itself. He is a scapegoat; he is also forgiveness. In the Gospel of John, Jesus' life is not taken; it is given: "...I lay down my life, that I may take it again. No one takes it from me, but I lay it down of my own accord. I have power to lay it down, and I have power to take it again." Mark's Jesus is the Lion of Judah, rushing courageously to Jerusalem but snared there where his last words were "Why have you forgotten me?" John's Jesus is in some ways the most down-to-earth, as when he weeps over Lazarus, makes wine in Cana, and washes the disciples' feet. He is also sublime, conquering thirst, blindness, paralysis, and even death. With eagle eyes he sees glory and eternity in the cross that he seems almost to mount like a throne, and from which he announces, "It is consummated." Mark the lion and John the eagle reveal the leonine and aquiline Christ: crucified Son of the earth and soaring Lord of the sky.

Water and Fire

Water is also crucial in Mark and John. Both books describe Jesus' baptism, which mystics have always understood as a sign of his humility, since he was innocent, and as the opposite of our own baptisms. Instead of washing away injustice, cruelty, dishonesty, and other "soul-diseases" from which we suffer, Jesus' baptism absorbs all those maladies. He turns poisoned water into life-water. He takes to it like a fish.

On a shelf in my bedroom, under Marc Chagall's painting,  "The White Crucifixion," I have a small fossil of a prehistoric fish. David Jones' long complex poem, *Anathemata,* eloquently celebrates Christ the *Ichthys,* the Fish, master of water that is death by drowning and life by drinking. Jones writes about the *ichthys*-sign stamped like my fossil on all creation from the beginning, from the breaking of the ice age glaciers over Britain (the breaking of the host over the chalice), to the worship of the mother goddess by prehistoric man, the mother of the Fish. Every hill in Britain, he says, and every tumid tumulus is a reminder of the pregnant virgin. The *ichthyic* sign was stamped on Hector, who was dragged around the walls of Troy and killed there, as Christ was dragged outside the walls of Jerusalem and killed, a fish out of water. Jones reminds us that our word "admiral" is an apt title for Christ: it comes from the Arabic *amir-ul bahri,* meaning "prince of the sea." That is the *Ichthys* Christ who walks on water and subdues a storm at sea.

How does fire show up in Jesus' life and words? True to his stark approach, Mark's references to fire are ominous warnings to those of us who resist or destroy life and love. John includes similar warnings, but he emphasizes Jesus as life-giving light.

> Helios may be a Greek god but the image of life-light streaming across the sky is also Jewish.

The Crystal Cave by Mary Stewart is the first in a trilogy of novels about the life of Merlin the magician. One of the first "tricks" Merlin learns from his master is to summon fire out of thin air. This mythic wizardry makes me yearn for the master of the fire of life and love: Jesus *Helios* Christ, the Radiant Dawn whom we praise in the Oh Antiphons. *Helios* may be a Greek God, but the image of life-light streaming across the sky is also Jewish: the prophet Ezekiel described the throne of God as a fiery chariot, the *merkabah,* whose wheels pointed in every direction, revealing God's freedom to enter, illuminate and enliven every corner of creation.

Here then is the Christ who captivates me in Advent, the master of all the four elements: earth, air, water and fire. He is the Lion, the Eagle, the Fish, the Admiral, and the Sun.

In the spirit of some of the first Christian poets, my Advent praise refrain is: We buried the Lion who made the earth, who clawed a way out of the pit. We smothered the Eagle who made the air, who hovers above the sea. We pierced the Fish who made the sea and out gushed a flood of life. We extinguished the Sun who made the stars, who then set fire to earth.

Christmas around the World

www.putumayo.com

Reflection by Tessa Bielecki

This global collection is my favorite Christmas music. It begins with shouts of "Merry Christmas" in four different languages and joyous music in the Haitian troubadour style, followed by "Here We Come-A-Wassailing" with ancient Celtic flavors from the violin, the Irish penny whistle and the "percussive pulse" of the *bodhran*.

I love *Adeste Fidelis* with a Cuban beat provided by bongos and congas and "Deck the Halls" as a Cuban *cha cha chá*. I soar to the sound of steel drums from Barbados ringing out "God Rest Ye Merry Gentlemen" with a riff that sounds like a gentle Caribbean rain. And I can't keep from stomping my feet to the accordion played by "The Cajun Queen" and then Michael Doucet's rousing Cajun version of "We Three Kings!" There are quieter moments in this collection, too: "White Christmas" sung in Spanish by Los Reyes, who come from the region of southern France known for its Gypsy rumba; a unique "Silent Night" played on the banjo and sung in exquisite French by Kali from Martinique; and "What Child Is This," an innovative instrumental by Dan Crary, one of today's most accomplished flatpicking guitarists.

Be sure to read the liner notes to learn more about Christmas customs from various cultures around the world and also their fascinating musical heritages. These range from Puerto Rican *aguinaldo* and Cuban *guajira* to Antillean *beguine*, rooted in *belle dance* with touches of European mazurkas and quadrilles. *Joyeux Noel*, *Feliz Navidad*, and Merry Christmas!

13

Feasting around the Globe

"…making spirits bright…"

Tessa Bielecki

After Midnight Mass on Christmas Eve, the French enjoy *réveillon*, a sumptuous meal of sausages, oysters, roast goose or turkey with *Bûche de Noel*, a cake shaped like a yule log. In some parts of the country, they eat thirteen different desserts!

Bulgarians bake a large round cake called *kravai*, decorated with a bird, a flower, a cross, topped with a burning candle. The mother and father of the family break a "good luck" piece from the ceremonial cake.

Rumanians love roast pig for Christmas dinner, served with a wheat loaf called *colaci* and a symbolic cake called *turta*, made of layers of thin dough shaped like leaves, representing the Christ-Child's swaddling clothes.

Serbians bake several coins into a circular loaf of bread. After one of the children recites the Lord's Prayer, everyone simultaneously breaks off a piece of bread. Those who get the coins are reminded not of worldly riches, but the richness of God's blessings. These coins are often contributed to the poor.

Venezuelans serve a festive ham bread and Scandinavians their *lutfisk*. Costa Ricans wrap their *tamales* in plantain leaves instead of corn tortillas. Brazilians begin Christmas Eve with a big *churrasco*, a barbeque, and then fireworks. The Polish, on the other hand, eat a mostly meat-free meal: beet soup, pickled herring, fried smelts, and jellied carp. The Germans also eat carp or goose and *stölen*, a fruited yeast bread. The Spanish prefer *pavo trufado de Navidad*, turkey stuffed with truffles: mushrooms, not chocolates!

Pink Pigs, *Ping Guo*, and Plum Pudding

Norwegians eat rice porridge on Christmas Eve, either as a meal for lunch or dessert after the evening meal. If you find an almond in your portion, you get a pink or white marzipan pig. Dinner on Christmas Day is pork or mutton with potatoes and cabbage cooked with caraway seeds and vinegar. Inuit peoples northwest of Norway in Greenland choose whale skin with a strip of blubber inside.

Chinese Christians give each other apples wrapped in colored paper. In China Christmas Eve is called *Ping An Ye*, "quiet or silent night." The word for apple is *ping guo*, which sounds similar.

In England and Ireland it is traditional to eat plum pudding decorated with a sprig of holly. There are no plums in the "pudding." (The English call most dried fruits "plums" and dessert "pudding.") G.K. Chesterton, the "King of Christmas," had such a passion for plum pudding that he called it "a permanent monument of human mysticism and human mirth." He was probably describing himself when he wrote, "I know a kind of person who finds one Christmas pudding a complete meal in itself, and even a little over. For my own part, I should say that three, or perhaps four, Christmas puddings might be said to constitute a complete meal.... Scientific theories change, but the plum-pudding remains the same, century after century."

On Christmas Eve, people in New Mexico eat *posole*,

a pre-Columbian Mexican soup or stew made with pork and hominy, and *biscochitos*, anise-cinnamon cookies. After *Las Posadas*, traditional foods include *tamales* and hot chocolate. (I spike mine with red chile.)

And don't forget the candy canes. What is the origin of this tradition? Many years ago, a candy maker wanted to create a sweet that symbolized the true meaning of Christmas: Jesus. The hard candy was shaped like a "J" to represent Jesus' name. The color white symbolizes his purity, and the color red the blood he shed for us. Recent studies show that smelling or tasting peppermint offers a quick pick-me-up. The aroma may have the same effect as a whiff of smelling salts. Peppermint tea will do the same, of course, without the sugar.

Making Spirits Bright

What about Christmas drinks? Turks and Finns serve coffee to their guests. Russians serve tea in glasses with lemon, candied ginger, mint leaves, and candied cherries studded with whole cloves.

The English serve mulled cider or wassail, made of ale or wine flavored with sugar, spices and roasted apples. Sometimes wassail is called lamb's wool because the pulp of the cooked apples looks frothy like lamb's wool. A *wassail* is not only a drink but a salutation, a drinking song or a carol sung by wassailers, or a toast to someone's good health. The word originally comes from the Anglo-Saxon *waeshaeil*, from the Old Norse *vesheill*, meaning "good health," or the more popular "cheers!"

The Swedes love glögg, originally mulled wine, now made stronger with brandy, vodka, or aquavit. Orange peel, raisins, whole cloves and cinnamon sticks are traditional. Cardamom pods add a unique flavor, juniper berries a fresh wintry aroma.

New Year's

What do you eat to ensure a prosperous New Year? The French eat pancakes, the Germans eat fish, Native Americans eat acorns and salmon. The Swiss eat whipped cream and drip some on the floor.

Hold your door wide open at midnight on New Year's Eve to let the spirit of the Old Year out and the New Year in. And pay attention to the weather on January 1. In an old Saxon manuscript we find, "If the *Kalends*, or first of January falls on…the moon's day, *Monday*, then there will be a severe and confused winter, a good spring, windy summer, and a rueful year with much sickness."

In Spain New Year's Eve is called *Nochevieja*, "Old Night." It is customary to eat twelve grapes with the twelve strokes of the clock, one grape for each month of the year. If you manage to eat all twelve grapes, you will be lucky in the coming year.

Greenlanders celebrate New Year's Eve twice: at 8 PM when the new year comes to Denmark and at 12 AM when it arrives in Greenland.

In Scotland, the first person to set foot in the house on New Year's Day affects the fortunes of the household. This custom is known as "first footing." Strangers bring good luck. Sometimes it's better if they are fair-haired, sometimes dark-haired.

Millions

Directed by Danny Boyle

foxsearchlight.com

Reflection by David Denny

*W*hen I was a kid in Koko-mo, Indiana, I had friends who were baseball fiends. They knew all kinds of stats and history. I was impressed, but puzzled. I didn't have that gene. I loved those pink slabs of bubble gum in waxy wrappers that included a baseball card. But I don't remember having much of a collection. I didn't memorize Willie Mays' batting average or save my allowance to buy rare cards at the local hobby shop. But I liked the sound of *Minnie Minoso*.

After first seeing *Millions*, I exited the theater and studied the publicity poster. One critic gave a perfect description of Damian, the freckle-faced star of the movie: this kid collected facts about the saints with the avidity American boys devote to baseball trivia.

We quickly learn that Maureen, the mother of Damian and his older brother Anthony, has recently died. Their father buys land in a new subdivision and the little family prepares to move out of the home that holds too many memories. It's late summer, and in the opening scene, the brothers race through fields of yellow flowers on their bikes to arrive at the raw land of their new home.

Moving involves lots of cardboard boxes and Damian hauls the empties out behind the housing development, using them to build a fort near the railroad tracks. He reads about the saints in all his spare time. On one of his first days in a new school, the teacher asks Damian's class whom they admire. Most mention soccer stars. Damian stands up and launches a litany. He loves St. Roch, and then there are the virgin martyrs.

He describes a couple of brutal martyrdoms, the kids are appalled, and the teacher silences Damian. But in his fort he is free to deepen his relationship with the saints, and soon they begin appearing. St. Clare chats with him about heaven as she smokes a cigarette. ("You can do whatever you want up there.") She blows excellent smoke rings.

At one point Damian's fort suffers serious damage, but lucky for him, St. Charles Lwanga and the Ugandan martyrs (feast day June 3, martyred in 1886—just ask Damian) happen to show up and put all in order. They also pray for rain. (When a friend asked me to describe this movie in a nutshell, I said it's Beaver Cleaver meets Charles Lwanga!)

> St. Clare chats with him about heaven as she smokes a cigarette.

The plot thickens when Christmas approaches and the English pound is about to change to the Euro. Damian comes into some big money. He is certain it is from God. So he sets about using it to help the poor, which includes buying pizzas for the homeless. With his new friend St. Nicholas, he stuffs pounds galore into his Mormon neighbors' mail slot. His brother Anthony has a more pragmatic, materialist outlook on their newfound wealth and Damian's extravagances confound and infuriate him.

Alas, the money is not exactly from God, and someone comes looking for it, a very creepy someone. But never fear: Sts. Peter and Joseph manage to lend helping hands, and although Damian must flee the Christmas pageant with Joseph and Mary's donkey, all is not lost. In the end, Damian has a chance to repay the good deed done by the Ugandan martyrs, and the true spirit of Christmas prevails.

This eccentric and funny movie, although steeped in Roman Catholic lore and legend, can appeal to any family. Far-fetched and zany as it is, it may spark some good conversations about what is most important in life, and what, in the end, is most real and true.

Dew and Ember

David Denny

He descended in March like dew upon the grass:
He came so still: a secret, tender tryst.
But now the waves of pain are coming fast,
And clouds, in labor, bleed; the old world twists

In anguish. Good news, yes, and yet it jars:
The Prince of Peace is born with warrior bones,
His seed was sown within the month of Mars,
He slips from the sheath a sword all strapped and honed.

God's passion, stripped of glory, sleeps on hay,
No, not like dew, but like an ember, glowing.
All who see him burn like fired clay,
Yet rise, like Phoenix, wild with love, and knowing

Good news, yes, for heaven's ours tonight:
The King comes clothed in flesh and powerless might.

Part 4
The New Year

Angels, as this year now nears its end
Fold their wings, as gently down they bend,
Rent and broken hopes on earth to mend.
May they find us ready to rise!

Angels, at the dawn of a New Year
Spread bright wings and rise, and rise from here
Raising us to heights we crave, yet fear.
May they find us daring!

David Steindl-Rast, O.S.B.

Love and joy come to you,
And to you your wassail too,
And God bless you, and send you
A happy new year.
Traditional Carol

The New Year is a good time to consider
what determines the rhythm of our lives. Different kinds of
calendars record different kinds of time. Our "Day-Timers"
help us chronicle what the Greeks called *chronos*, clock time,
the precisely measured minutes and hours that we fill with work.
But we may have gardening calendars that remind us of the
rhythms of seeds and harvests. Our liturgical calendars remind
us of the rhythms of fast and feast: of Lent and Easter, Advent
and Christmas, and "ordinary time" in between.

I grew up learning to distinguish between feast days and
"ferial" days, the ordinary days which make each festal day that
much more special. In *The Supper of the Lamb*, a cookbook
full of profound theology (or is it a theological book full of
recipes?), Episcopal priest Robert Farrar Capon wrote: "Let us
[live] festally first of all, for life without occasions is not worth
living. But ferially, too, for life is so much more than occasions,
and the grand ordinariness must never go unsavored."

How do we learn to celebrate what the Greeks called *kairos*, an intersection of now and eternity, a kind of timeless time that cannot be measured in minutes? *Kairos* is about meaning, not minutes; ecstasy, not efficiency; consummation, not consumption. Poetry helps us find our way into this *kairos*, as do prayer, ritual, ceremony, and love.

Begin this New Year by lighting new candles and walking through a doorway. The New Year is also a good time to bless new calendars, reminding ourselves that "all days are for celebration and contemplation, for giving and receiving love."

In the Roman Catholic tradition, January 1 is also the feast of the Motherhood of Mary, a good day not only to honor the one we call *the* Blessed Mother, but *all* blessed mothers who live out the mysticism of motherhood.

The Bible's Book of Revelation provides a good meditation for the New Year: "The world of the past has gone... Now I am making the whole of creation new" (Rev. 21:4-5).

—Tessa Bielecki

A Celtic Blessing

May the blessings of God
be with you
ever and always.
May the Christ-Child
light the road before you
every night and day.
May God take
the harm of the year
away from you.

Glad Tidings for the New Year

We are all meant to be mothers of God.
Meister Eckhart

Mother is the name for God in the lips and hearts of little children.
William Makepeace Thackeray

Mothers are the ones who carry children for nine months. They are the ones who learn to sleep on their backs.... They are the ones who sweat, push, and cry out for pain in the labor room. Dads pass out cigars. Mothers are the ones who spend hours spooning out jars of strained apricots.... Dads lunch at the Racquet Club. Joseph never passed out cigars or lunched at the Nazareth Racquet Club, but you can be sure he appreciated what Mary went through as a mother.
D.L. Stewart

It's left to our imagining to square
The rigors of the manger with the crèche,
To hear the muffled cry, to mark the stretch
And push a birthing God might bring to bear.
The image of the crèche is sweet and light,
But, Lord, was there no blood to sweat that night?
Christopher Fitzgerald

Mary was not asked to lead a special kind of life, to retire to the temple and live as a nun, to cultivate suitable virtues or to claim special privileges.... The one thing that [God] did ask of her was the gift of her humanity.... She was to give him her daily life.
Caryll Houslander

O Christ, what shall we offer you coming on earth? Angels offer praise, Heaven lights up a star, Magi bring gifts, shepherds their wonder, earth a cave, desert a manger. We offer you a Mother.
Author Unknown

Walking through the Door

A Ritual for the New Year

Compiled by Tessa Bielecki

All: The world of the past has gone.... I know all about you; and now I have opened in front of you a door that nobody will be able to close. (Rev. 21:4; 3:8)

Reader: *A Reading from the Book of Revelation on the Threshold of the New Year*

The world of the past has gone.... I saw a new heaven and a new earth.... Then the one sitting on the throne spoke: "Now I am making the whole of creation new," he said. "Write this: That what I am saying is sure and will come true." And then he said, "It is already done. I am the Alpha and the Omega, the Beginning and the End." (Rev. 21: 1-6)

All: The world of the past has gone.... I know all about you; and now I have opened in front of you a door that nobody will be able to close. (Rev. 21:4; 3:8)

Left: I am the Alpha and the Omega, who is, who was, and who is to come. (Rev. 1:8)

Right: If anyone has ears to hear, let him listen to what the Spirit is saying. (Rev. 2:7)

L: He has the key of David, so that when he opens, nobody can close, and when he closes, nobody can open. (Rev. 3:7)

R: I know all about you; and now I have opened in front of you a door that nobody will be able to close. (Rev. 3:8)

L: I am standing at the door, knocking. If one of you hears me calling and opens the door, I will come in to share your meal, side by side with you. (Rev. 3:20)

R: What matters is for you to become altogether new. (Galatians 6:15)

L: Your mind must be "renewed" by a spiritual revolution so that you can put on the new self that has been created in God's way, in the goodness and holiness of truth. (Ephesians 4:23)

R: All I can say is that I forget the past and I strain ahead for what is still to come. (Philippians 3:13)

All: The world of the past has gone.... I know all about you; and now I have opened in front of you a door that nobody will be able to close. (Rev. 21:4; 3:8)

(Move to the most important door in your home or to a symbolic passageway.)

All: To focus on the door is to recall our responsibility to cross its threshold. To pass through the door is to remember the Source of new life.

L: Source of Life, Creator of time and history, be for us the true Door.

R: Be for us the true Door, which you open for us.

L: Be for us the Door which leads us into Mystery.

R: Be with us as we take our first steps into the New Year.

L: May this year be a time of reconciliation between peoples, a time of peace among nations.

R: May it be a time when swords are beaten into ploughshares, and the clash of arms gives way to songs of peace.

L: May we live this New Year listening to the voice of the Holy Spirit.

R: May we purify our memories and acknowledge our failings.

L: May dialogue between the followers of the great religious traditions expand, and include those who are disillusioned with those traditions.

R: May all people discover the joy of our oneness so we may have life and have it abundantly.

L: You know all about us and care for us.

R: You have opened in front of us a door that nobody will be able to close.

All: To focus on the door is to recall our responsibility to cross its threshold. To pass through the door is to remember the Source of new life.

(Walk through the door or symbolic passageway.)

An Irish Blessing for the New Year

May you find truth in the year's smallest grace
And hope in the year's most heavy cross.
May the pillar of light before your face
Drive off the darkness so you're never lost.
May your journey be safe where'er you go
And angels protect you from hassle and fuss.
May you learn to walk a little bit slow
And to grow each day in hope and in trust.
And may the God of new beginnings
Grant you a new year of love and peace.

A Calendar Blessing for the New Year

Gather your calendars for the New Year and bless them in whatever way is sacred to you. Then you may want to recite these prayers, originally written by Sr. Carmela of the Holy Spirit and adapted by Tessa Bielecki.

Maker of the universe, you who fashioned the sun to rule by day and the moon by night, you who live beyond time and reside in the imperishable moment, we ask your blessing this New Year upon your gift to us of time.

Bless our calendars, these ordered lists of days, weeks and months, of holy days, fasts and feasts. May they remind us that all days are for celebration and contemplation, for giving and receiving love.

Bless this New Year, each of its three hundred and sixty-five days and nights. Bless us with peace and joy. And grant to us the New Year's gift of a year of love. Amen.

O You, "in whom we live and move and have our being," I see this New Year as a blank page that you are giving me, upon which you will write day by day what you will give me. With full confidence I am writing at the top of the page from now on: "Do with me what you will." And at the bottom I have already put my "Amen" to every disposition of your divine will. "Yes," I say "yes" to all the joys, all the sorrows, all the graces, to all the hardships you will reveal to me day by day. Let my "Amen" always be followed by "Alleluia," uttered with all my heart in the joy of perfect giving. Give me your love and your grace and I shall be rich enough.

14

The Mysticism of Motherhood

A Woman Wrapped in Silence

Tessa Bielecki

One of the greatest gifts any married couple can give a celibate friend or relative is the privilege of sharing the experience of natural childbirth. My own brother and sister-in-law, Tom and Karen, blessed me abundantly years ago when they invited me to participate in the birth of their second child, Mark Francis. I prepared myself by attending birth classes with Karen, reading baby books she gave me, and meditating on the mystery of motherhood magnificently portrayed by John Lynch in his Marian classic, *A Woman Wrapped in Silence*.

I read this book every Advent. It's one of those classics that goes on living, inspiring and nourishing me. Lynch is a genius and a lyrical poet, a theologian who demonstrates the unity of poetry and theology, very evident in the early centuries of the Church but sometimes lacking in our scientific age.

Tender Human Touches

I find *A Woman Wrapped in Silence* as rich and inspired as Holy Scripture, a well of such wisdom, it will take me innumerable meditative readings over a lifetime to plumb the depths. Lynch picks up where the Gospel leaves off. He fills in all those tender human touches we hope were there. The silences in scripture are many, the sentences short, and the words meagre: "What source we have of knowledge of the days is sparing, and has left us many days still veiled...We must have more to lead us where our love would seek to go." Lynch is careful to keep his book within the limits of the facts in the Christian Testament. Yet he still manages to unveil those days the Gospel shrouds in silent mystery.

Christians consider the Gospel of Luke the Marian Gospel. Because it contains so many details we don't find in the other stories, tradition tells us that Mary revealed the details to Luke alone. I am convinced that Mary herself revealed even more to John Lynch through his own mystical experience, transcending the boundaries of space and the limitations of time. Lynch somehow participates in the life of Mary and tells us what he sees and hears. In his grasp of feminine psychology, he reveals what it feels like to be a woman, a wife, and mother. He doesn't merely describe the experience of Mary, Joseph and Jesus. The lyrical language he uses evokes the same experience in his reader. I seldom recommend a book as passionately as I do *A Woman Wrapped in Silence*.

Motherhood and Fatherhood

As my friend David Levin said many years ago on the feast of the Holy Family, parenthood is not what you do if you don't have a religious vocation. Parenthood is a significant vocation in itself, although it is sometimes undervalued. We need to uphold the miracle and mysticism of motherhood and homemaking. And we need renewed sensitivity to the mystery of motherhood unfolding in union with the mystery of fatherhood.

We cannot consider the motherhood of Mary without the fatherhood of Joseph, who was not a mere appendage hovering silently in the background. Joseph played a pivotal role as Mary's spouse. One flaw in the liturgical calendar is the omission of St. Joseph's feast during the Christmas season. We celebrate Stephen, the first martyr, John, the disciple whom Jesus loved, the Holy Innocents, and the Motherhood of Mary. How unfortunate not to celebrate St. Joseph as well, since Mary could not have managed without him.

> *Home is like a womb to us, but the time comes when life requires us to leave the comfort of the womb and enter a wider world.*

Joseph was not merely Mary's protector. He was her beloved husband. Lynch gives beautiful descriptions of their relationship: "She'd made a bond with Joseph...It came to her that this content, this ease, this quiet in her was not of the hills, or roofs, or streets that were her childhood's paths, but was of Joseph. Joseph was her peace. He was her home, and holding her now, his name was warm and strong and innocent of fears. She could be confident of him, she could be glad for Joseph." Mary doesn't focus on the utilitarian service Joseph can provide for her but rejoices in him. During their wedding procession, walking beside him, she watches "the longer shadow that his figure made ahead of her," and trustingly she moves beside him because she knows "his arm for strong protection," but even more, she knows "his heart for harbor."

Homeland for the Heart

Lynch makes the love of Mary and Joseph come alive. They hold hands and embrace one another. They weep and laugh together. Joseph sees in Mary what others can't because they don't know her well enough. Every chance he gets, when she's not looking at him, Joseph sneaks a peek at her: walking down the street, leaning pensively against a door, kneeling

to stoke the fire. And Mary sneaks peeks at him, too: "She'd grown to know this air and attitude that graced him here, when unobserved she saw him standing by the road. It was the sharp, unconscious profile of his eagerness, and all the gift of him that she'd received so many times. She'd learned this light that rested on his face, and seen before the lift his head made when he watched for her."

Spousal Love

On their terrible flight into Egypt, Mary can't keep her eyes off Joseph as they make camp the first night: "And when he saw her eyes that followed him and did not turn until he'd moved beyond the light, he guessed of how much more he was than one who gathered sticks and spoke with her. He knew he was a homeland for her heart, a wide, wide acre where she was not strange." These are eloquent descriptions of a great spousal love relationship: Mary was glad for Joseph who was her peace, her home, her harbor, "a homeland" for her own heart.

The first dramatic dimension of seeing my new little nephew being born was the intimacy between Tom and Karen throughout labor and delivery. Mary and Joseph had to know the same loving closeness. Just as Karen couldn't have delivered Mark without Tom, so Mary could not have raised Jesus without Joseph's love.

Mary, Maternal Mystic

Lynch beautifully describes Mary's "maternal ministry," "the brief sweet offices of motherhood," the "cares that were for her but cares for Him," her son: communion with her baby "in a kiss upon his brow," the "instinctive comforting in gesture and in soft maternal murmurs," the "love that lifts to lullaby" because it is "a mother's need to sing." He doesn't talk about nursing Jesus at the breast, the messy diapers and the sleepless nights when the crying wouldn't stop, but we can assume it.

A Woman Wrapped in Silence presents Mary as the model mystic. It's refreshing to see a married mystic for a change instead of all those celibates like St. Teresa, who levitated instead of keeping her feet on the ground like Mary did! Mary shows us the essence of the spiritual life: she simply lived at all times in the presence of Christ. She was pure of heart because she willed only one thing. She was "hungered of a single need" and "sharpened to one clear and edged perception": God moved near her.

Does Mary do anything special or engage in any special spiritual practices? No, she simply goes about her business, the business of motherhood and homemaking. As Lynch says:

> *There was not overmuch of speech...This household set, unsigned and undistinguished with some others on a village hill, moved on as other village households moved. A fire to tend, and earthenware to scour, lamps to trim and keep, and threads to draw, while old words fell...about the morning blue, and of the rains. But old worn words were not as others spoke...And usual tasks were silhouette against awareness, flaming like a constant light that haloed with its own significance the cares that were for her but cares for Him. To come. To go. To pull the shutters in. To mark the daybreak hour and dark.*

The secret of Mary's mysticism is simple: "usual tasks are silhouette against awareness." The secret of contemplative life is to recognize that the ordinary tasks of our everyday existence are carried out in the presence of God. This is the only kind of religious life that matters to me: a life of *earthy* mysticism and incarnational worldliness.

> Karen cut the umbilical cord herself to symbolize the first big letting go, the first break with baby.

And this I believe is the most radical consequence of the Incarnation, so radical that after over two thousand years, we've hardly begun to believe it. Whenever we love and take care of our spouses and children, neighbors and friends, we love and care for Christ. Here's how Lynch puts it: "She knelt and held him close against her heart, and in the midnight, adoration fused with human love, and was not separate."

Letting Go

After the loving intimate at-one-ment of mother and father in the act of giving birth, what impressed me next in the experience of my nephew's birth was the excruciating pain that Karen suffered. It was harder for me than for Tom. Since he was the coach and had to help Karen focus on her breathing, he was able to be more detached. But I had no official function (except to keep those rosary beads rattling in the background!), so not only could I see the pain, I was compelled to enter into every trembling moment of it. I found it more difficult than I expected.

One baby book Karen gave me to prepare insisted that pain serves a purpose: each contraction is not only another pain but another effort of the uterus to open to allow the baby to enter the world. Pregnancy and birth thus provide a paradigm for the essence of motherhood: the nurturing of life. But Karen helped me see another important dimension of the paradigm: from the very beginning, as well as at the end, motherhood nurtures life through a painful generous process of letting go.

This is what I absorbed most from the experience of Mark's birth. Karen cut the umbilical cord herself. Weeks before her delivery, she explained how she wanted to cut the cord to symbolize the first big letting go, the first break with baby, the first of many separations.

In the first, the baby is ready to be born and leaves the womb. No wonder new mothers suffer "post-partum blues" after childbirth! The first tragic separation of motherhood has occurred. The blues occur over and over again as life goes on because life and love require more and more separations. When the baby is ready to be weaned, he leaves the breast. Another wrenching. And then the worst wrench of all: the child is grown and leaves the home.

No Shelter from Pain and Loneliness

In a passage about this stage which separates mother and child, Mary and Jesus, Lynch compares the portents stirring heavily in the air, compelling Jesus to be about his mission, to the stirring of the baby preparing to leave the womb. Home is like a womb to us, but the time comes when life requires us to leave the comfort of that womb and enter a wider world.

When the time came, Mary let go of Jesus. As Lynch reveals, she had waited for this too long to find that any press of pain was "stranger" to her: "She'd lived this day and learned the feel of it." Only the loneliness was new: "loneliness that corners at last upon our hearts, close woven in the thread of human love."

"She could not cling to him in tears, nor give him other than a freedom glad for roads and towns, nor seek to be about his feet and slow them to her needs." Mary had to let go and look at Jesus as more than her son: "He had gone out to distances, to time, He'd stepped beyond possession, hers or his, or Nazareth's.... She knew he was a child who answered to another claim than hers." A mother suffers when a child leaves home. Lynch presents this as the most painful letting go, more painful than the initial act of giving birth. But, like childbirth, this, too, is bearable pain: "He had not sheltered her from pain, nor even asked she not be free to know our anguish...And he'd not softened any loneliness when Nazareth was ended. She was free to sorrow...she need not ever turn from grief."

Madonna to Life, Madonna to Death

There is yet another separation worse than leaving home. Not every mother knows it, but many do, like Mary, like my own mother who knew it twice, like women all over the world, and that is letting go of a child through death, not only being "madonna to life," but "madonna to death." Here is where the mystery of letting go on behalf of life becomes its most mystical.

This is a somber conclusion. But today the mystery of motherhood unfolds in a somber world of war, exploitation, and the threat of nuclear disaster. Brother David Steindl-Rast, O.S.B. raised these issues in one of his Christmas letters and urged us to find the methods we need to deal with our global crises. His first suggestion was that we all become more motherly!

"That's all I can think of: face the enormous task, find one small thing I can do, and do it with a mother's dedication," Brother David wrote. "That way, at the very moment when time is running out on us, the fullness of time can break in. Because it is under the image of mother and child that we celebrate this fullness of time."

Christmas happened first when Mother Mary's time, like Karen's, was "fulfilled" and she gave birth. Christmas will keep happening again and again, here and now in our broken world, the moment we mother the child within us, the moment we mother our own world.

The
Story
Teller

David Denny

Children, there was a girl
She lived in a small village
On a tall dry mesa the size of ours.
She did what you do.
But her ears heard more than sounds.
You hear me talk
And know I am bigger than my words:
They come from inside me.
This girl heard a word,
But it wasn't inside her.
She was inside the word.

She stayed as still as the
Stone canyon walls,
And let herself be spoken.

That word, which made
The desert and the sky,
The mesas and the arroyos,
The rain and the girl
That great word of our Grandfather
Loved the girl
And became so small
He lived inside her
As you lived inside your mother once.

What became of that Word-Boy
Is another story.
Today, simply listen.
She is your mother, and
Gives you special ears
To hear more than sounds,
More than coyotes,
Rain, thunder
And wind.
You will hear your name,
And you will know what you must do.

You will walk in beauty,
Laugh and weep in beauty,
Because the girl is beauty
And your mother,
The Mother of Millions,
From a tall dry mesa
The size of ours.

Mother of God Similar to Fire

Icons by William Hart McNichols,
Reflections by Mirabai Starr

Maryknoll, NY: Orbis Books, 2010

Reflection by Tessa Bielecki

"People of all faiths call her Mother," writes Mirabai Starr in her introduction to this book of icons and reflections. "In moments of deeply personal sorrow, we turn to her for consolation. In our bewilderment, we turn to her for insight."

Starr describes Mary not only as our personal Mother but as Mother of the World. "When the world seems to be losing its balance and spiraling into a vortex of violence and greed, we turn to Mary for a reminder of what matters most, what endures when all else seems lost, what grace may yet be available when we meet fear with love."

The icons of William Hart McNichols manifest this global dimension: Mother of God, She Who Hears the Cries of the World; The Andronicus Icon of the Mother of God, Consoler of Women; Mary Most Holy, Mother of all Nations, who holds our planet viewed from space against her golden robe.

McNichols' iconography is unusual, mystical, full of bright colors and rich symbols: snow and stars, water and fire, trees and chalice. There are traditional icons and more contemporary ones, Mary as Burning Bush, the nursing Mary, and several black madonnas, including Mother and Child of Kibeho, where Mary and the baby are clearly African.

"You gaze on the icon, but it gazes on you too.... We need to gaze on truly conversational, truly loving images, images that will return our love," says McNichols. As he explains in his Preface, Starr's meditative prayers are deliberately brief and serve as an opening for each of us who read them. The book offers "a contemplative space for you to enter and find your own relationship with the images and words."

This was certainly my own experience, since I find the icons and contemplative reflections deeply and soulfully connected, as are the icon-painter and the writer of the reflections, who are friends and neighbors in New Mexico.

This well-designed volume features fifty-one sumptuous icons and prayers for only $25. I heartily commend Orbis Books for such generosity.

At the end of the book a fiercely red mushroom cloud looms over The Triumph of the Immaculate Heart and Mirabai Starr prays: "You who radiate peace, dear Mary, help us to break this obsession with war and vanquish the culture of death."

The final icon shows an aged Mary as the Risen Christ appears to her. Starr's final prayer openly addresses the tragedy of today's scandals in our churches and communities: "Beloved Mother…The House of God is on fire. Powerful men, once helpless, perpetuate the cycle of violence and violate helpless children." Then, like Mary and her Son and the spirit of his Gospel, this prayer and the book's reflections end on a note of deep hope, and once again with global perspective: "[L]et new life spring from the death now unfolding: a new house, built on love, its doors flung open to all the world." Surely this is the message of every Christmas as we celebrate the birth of Jesus, sprung from the dark mystery of Mother Mary's womb.

My own favorite icons are the simplest and most modern-looking ones. Mary of the Magnificat, Mother of the Poor spreads the folds of her cloak to give us refuge in our "work and worry," struggling "just to bring home a few eggs, a stack of tortillas," and "a few gallons of gas for a car that barely runs."

Both Mother of the Incarnate Word and *Nuestra Señora de Las Nieves,* Our Lady of the Snows, are "pregnant with the Word of God," that "miracle ripening in [Mary's] womb…within the mysterious heart of deep winter." May we, too, carry the Prince of Peace in our own soul-wombs this season, and then bear "the Sun of Justice into our midst."

A Wreath of Christmas Legends

Phyllis McGinley
New York: MacMillan,
1964, 1966, 1967, 1974

Reflection by Tessa Bielecki

I savor *A Wreath of Christmas Legends* every year during the Twelve Days. Phyllis McGinley retells fifteen medieval legends of the first Christmas in poetry beautifully illustrated with simple line drawings by Leonard Weisgard.

These legends answer some provocative questions: Why is the stork the patron of babies? Why is the robin's breast red? Why is the pine tree always green? Why does the owl wake at night? Why does the cat settle by the fire, "singing...household hosannahs like a pulsing kettle"? I love the "Canticle of the Bees," a song that can only be heard on Christmas Eve by the pure of heart.

My personal favorite is the "Ballad of the Rosemary," which describes why this herb is sacred, both aromatic and blue: on the way to Egypt, the Virgin Mary hung her wet laundry on a generous rosemary bush!

> *But when the clothes were wholesome,*
> *Where could she hang them all?*
> *"The lily breaks beneath them,*
> *The lilac stands too tall."*
> *So on the trembling rosemary*
> *She laid them one by one,*
> *And strong the rosemary held them*
> *All morning to the sun.*

"I thank you, gentle Rosemary.
Henceforward you shall bear
Blue clusters for remembrance
Of this blue cloak I wear;

"And not your blossoms only,
I give you as reward,
But where His raiment clung to you
Which clad the little Lord,

"All shall be aromatic,"
Said Mary, "for I bless
Leaf, stem, and flower
That from this hour
Shall smell of holiness."

Alas, this tiny volume, originally published by Macmillan in the late 1960s, is now out of print. But it's well worth hunting for it in stores that sell used books. (One year I found five copies for family and friends.)

This collection of poems is not only warm and delightful for young and old alike; its deeper meanings inspire us and move our hearts. We come to understand how all creation mysteriously participated in the first Nativity. And we awaken to the mystical possibility that everything in the universe still vibrates to the magic of Christmas.

The holly! the holly! oh, twine it with bay—
Come give the holly a song;
For it helps to drive stern winter away,
With his garment so sombre and long...
Then sing to the holly, the Christmas holly,
That hangs over peasant and king;
While we laugh and carouse 'neath its glittering boughs,
To the Christmas holly we'll sing.

Eliza Cook

James Taylor at Christmas

jamestaylor.com,
columbiarecords.com

Reflection by David Denny

*W*hen I graduated from high school, James Taylor had just released "Fire and Rain." I have admired his work ever since. This collection contains Christmas classics, both sacred and secular. In secular songs like "Jingle Bells," Taylor goofs off with a funky groove and bluesy riffs that might make you laugh. If it doesn't, then his coy duet with Natalie Cole on "Baby, It's Cold Outside" will do the trick. He handles other standards with respect and warmth. His voice has the ease of twentieth-century crooners, but that mellow timbre expresses peace after a storm rather than escape from reality.

As for the sacred songs, "Go Tell it on the Mountain" reminds me that Taylor grew up walking country roads in Gospel territory. "In the Bleak Midwinter" is perhaps my favorite Christmas song, and Taylor sounds at home with the mystical Christology of Christina Rossetti's lyrics. "Some Children See Him" and "Who Comes this Night" are new to me. Both celebrate children's wonder and show that Christmas still inspires soulful melodic responses to the Incarnation. "Some see him lily white…bronzed and brown…almond-eyed…dark as they…"

One test of whether a Christmas album is worth buying is whether or not it moves you in June. For me, this recording passes the test. It is not a holiday novelty. A music critic reminded me that after the shocks, rage and discontent in response to the sixties' assassinations, the Vietnam War, racial and campus violence, Taylor's voice emerged as a calming, healing presence. Taylor had battled his own demons and emerged scarred but capable of expressing beauty, humor, and hope. I hear that tone ringing through these melodies.

A Winter Garden
Loreena McKennitt

www.quinlanroad.com

Loreena McKennitt has a unique and fascinating voice. This is a short collection with only five songs, including "Coventry Carol," a lament for the Holy Innocents slaughtered by "Herod, the king in his raging." "Good King Wenceslas" has a strong medieval Celtic feel.

Although "God Rest Ye Merry Gentlemen" is an old English carol, McKennitt's version has a distinctly Middle Eastern sound. The haunting strings and pipes suggest a camel caravan moving across desert sands. And no one pronounces "Tidings of comfort and joy" quite like Loreena.

It's hard to make out the lyrics to "Snow," originally a poem by Archibald Lampman, so the liner notes are crucial: "Like some soft minister of dreams, the snow-fall hoods me round; in wood and water, earth and air, a silence everywhere."

Wassail! Wassail!
Early American Christmas Music

www.revels.org

The Christmas Revels, founded and directed by John Langstaff, joyously interweave song, dance, drama, and verse in lively performances every Christmas in various locations around the country. Each year the program differs and combines professional principals, an amateur chorus, and the voices of the audience.

This production, with a glorious brass ensemble, tambourines, and tympani, includes the "Huron Indian Carol," "Go Tell it on the Mountain," and the "Cherry Tree Carol." Robert Lurtsema gives stirring readings of Carl Sandburg's "Star Silver" and an Iglulik

Eskimo poem. Jean Ritchie tells a touching Christmas tree story from her *Singing Family of the Cumberlands*. We hear but cannot see clog dancers from the Appalachian Mountains. One of my personal favorites is "Children, Go Where I Send Thee," accompanied by a wild soprano saxophone.

The Shaker song, "I Will Bow and Be Simple," is quietly meditative, "Wondrous Love" almost unbearably sublime, and "Shall We Gather at the River" a rousing finale.

One Holy Night
Red Nativity
www.brulerecords.com

Paul LaRoche and Robby Bee take traditional Christmas carols and blend them with Native American arrangements and style, adding drums, rattles, flute, and Lakota chants, and playing the music in minor keys.

There may be too much synthesizer. The "orchestration" may be less sophisticated than our other selections here. Sometimes the songs may seem chaotic with the chants superimposed on them. But Red Nativity has created something unique in "One Holy Night," considered the first Native American Christmas recording.

"O Come Emmanuel" and the Our Father become "Wakan Tanka's Prayer." The "Little Drummer Boy" becomes "Young Rain Drummer" with peals of thunder, a rain stick, rattles, and "bells" that sound like rain. "We Three Kings" becomes "Three Shaman" with pulsating rhythms that sound like the hooves of horses. (Listen for their neighing.)

I love hearing "Amazing Grace" sung in Lakota. And I can't resist this feathered Indian Madonna, painted by King Kuka from the Blackfeet Nation of Montana.

(Three reflections by Tessa Bielecki)   141

The Peace Album

Paul Horn

cdbaby.com

Reflections by David Denny

Paul Horn's "Inside the Taj Mahal" appeared in 1968, and I found it bewitchingly ethereal. Flute notes glided like birds around the Taj Mahal's dome, doubling back on each other in long tapering sinuations. It is moving now to listen to "The Peace Album," with solo flute renditions of familiar carols and pieces by Bach and Palestrina. New technology allowed Horn to lay down tracks that remind me of "Inside," but the Taj Mahal's magic acoustics are unreproducible.

This recording is just right for candlelight on a cold winter's night. It calms me down and wakes me up. Both meditation and playing the flute focus on breathing, and the "breathy" quality of Horn's solo flute embodies the resonance between respiration and inspiration.

Superstar R&B Christmas

Various Artists

Amazon.com (if you're lucky)

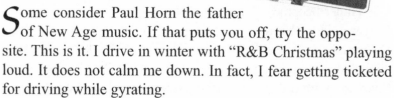

Some consider Paul Horn the father of New Age music. If that puts you off, try the opposite. This is it. I drive in winter with "R&B Christmas" playing loud. It does not calm me down. In fact, I fear getting ticketed for driving while gyrating.

It's an odd mixture, including serious Mahalia Jackson and Sarah Vaughan. These recordings are sometimes plain substandard. I try to think of it as "vintage." And they're informal. As for a favorite, it's The Miracles' "We Three Kings."

The Nativity Story

Directed by Catherine Hardwicke

www.thenativitystory.com,
www.newline.com

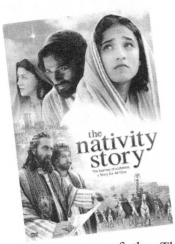

Reflection by Tessa Bielecki

I watch this film close to Epiphany every year because it sums up the whole saga of the Nativity. And I love the vivid portrayal of the Three Wise Men, who are clearly Persian Magi. I'm fascinated by their vast library of scrolls and the "telescope" they use to study the "star," which is really a convergence of three significant heavenly bodies. The story juxtaposes the Magi's camel journey across the desert with Mary and Joseph's donkey journey to Bethlehem, all of them finally meeting in the cave where Jesus is born.

The cast is outstanding. Soulful Palestinian actress Hiam Abbas is the mother of Mary, perplexed by her pregnant daughter, played by Keisha Castle-Hughes, the "whale-rider" from New Zealand.

Shohreh Aghdashloo, as beautiful as her Iranian name, is a stunning cousin Elizabeth, Alexander Siddiq a unique angel Gabriel, and Cieran Hinds a perfect Herod, the Roman pawn, with his oiled and carefully coiffed hair and beard.

The scenes of daily life in ancient Israel, filmed in Morocco and Italy, are captivating and colorful: shepherding, milking and making cheese, weaving and tanning, picking olives and herbs, baking flat bread and drawing water from the well. Of course we see Joseph the Carpenter with his tools.

The director gives a realistic portrayal of Nazareth shunning Mary as an unwed mother and the tenderness of Mary's relationship with Joseph. The young couple is shy with one another. On their long journey to Bethlehem, they finally come to know and love each other through shared struggle and hardship. (Pay attention to Joseph's feet.) When Jesus is born in a scene of realistic labor pains, Mary weeps and Joseph laughs. Then he, too, collapses in tears. Oscar Isaac plays a kind Joseph, young and virile, instead of an older protector.

The film uses traditional Christmas music well. I confess that I found this tale disappointing and sentimental when I first saw it in the theater. But I've grown to love it more and more as I continue to watch it at home as an annual part of my Twelve Days of Christmas.

Mary, Mother of God,
we are the poor soil
and the dry dust,
we are hard with a cold frost.
Be warmth to the world,
be the thaw,
warm on the cold frost
be the thaw that melts,
That the tender shoot of Christ,
piercing the hard heart,
flower to a spring in us.

Caryll Houselander

Part 5
Epiphany

Oh, far away in time they rode
Upon their wanderings,
And still in story goes abroad
The riding of the Kings.

Eleanor Farjeon

They lookéd up and saw a star,
Shining in the east beyond them far.
And to the earth, it gave great light.
And so they continued both day and night.
Noel, Noel, Noel, Noel, born is the King of Israel.
Traditional Carol

Epiphany is a lavish feast with a shining star,

splendid kings, shimmering gold, and the scents of exotic spices. In the Middle Ages it was called "the supreme day." Traditionally celebrated on January 6, Epiphany is older in origin than Christmas and began as the feast of Jesus' Nativity, also commemorating the visit of the Magi.

The name of the day comes from the Greek *epiphaneia*, meaning "manifestation." In the Greco-Roman world, an *epiphaneia* was an official state visit when a leader publicly showed himself to his people. The Christian feast of Epiphany means the manifestation of Jesus as Christ or Savior to the "Gentiles," to those beyond his own Jewish people, to all nations around the world.

On this feast we remember the journey of the Three Kings following the star, symbol of our own journey. We meditate on the meaning of the three gifts to the Christ-Child (did he really prefer the camel?) and the symbolism of the star. We bless gold, frankincense, myrrh, and chalk to mark the lintels of our doorways, blessing our homes and all who enter them in the coming year.

Jasper Winn writes about "Tracking the Magi," finding their traces in Iran through explorer Marco Polo. In Lark Ellen Gould's "Scents of Time and Place," we learn how contemporary Omanis gather frankincense today the same hard way their ancestors did for centuries along the Frankincense Trail.

According to G.K. Chesterton, "The midst of the earth is a raging mirth / And the heart of the earth a star." Raging mirth? Yes, but only if we take responsibility for our part in waging war. Frank Horne, part of the Harlem Renaissance, wrote his poem about the Magi in 1942 during the insanity of World War II. Decades later, his words become a sobering Epiphany mandate: "…as the bombs crash all over the world today, the real wise guys know that we've all got to go chasing stars again."

—*Tessa Bielecki*

At Christmas we celebrate the coming of the Magi, or Wise Men, who came to offer their gifts to the Infant Jesus.… May we not see in these wise men the representatives of the other [world] religions who bring their gifts to Christ… Could we not say that the Hindus offer the gift of gold, of interior religion, of the pure heart in which is found the presence of God? The Muslim can be seen to offer the gift of frankincense, the incense of the prayer of adoration, of worship which the Muslims offer five times daily to the one supreme God. The Buddhist can be seen to offer the gift of myrrh, the symbol of suffering and death, the sign that this world is passing away and that our destiny lies beyond the grave with the risen Christ.

—*Bede Griffiths*

Glad Tidings for Epiphany

Three Wise Women
Would have…
Asked directions,
Arrived on time,
Helped to deliver the baby,
Cleaned the stable,
Made a casserole,
Brought practical gifts and
There would be
Peace on Earth.
Author Unknown

Look at the stars! look, look up at the skies!
O look at all the fire-folk sitting in the air.
Gerard Manley Hopkins

The Star of Christmas means that the Son of God has turned the terrible night of our darkness, our anxiety and hopelessness into a Holy Night.
Karl Rahner, S.J.

You shine like a star, O Jesus, protecting me from shipwreck.
St. Faustina

Nothing will frighten me, neither wind nor rain, nor the dark clouds that come and hide the Star of Love. I know that beyond the clouds the bright Star still shines on.
St. Thérèse of Lisieux

You have guided me on a long, dark road, stony and hard, how often the strength seemed to have gone from me; and I despaired of ever seeing the light. But when my heart sickened in the depths of sorrow, a star arose before me, and I followed.
Edith Stein

15

Epiphany Splendor

"…a star, a star, shining in the night…"

Tessa Bielecki

Epiphany is my favorite day in the whole year. The traditional reading from Isaiah for this feast helps explain why. It revels in brightness and dawn, camels and dromedaries, gold, incense, and song and includes one of the greatest lines in the Jewish Testament: "You will grow radiant, your heart throbbing and full." I love the alliteration of *throbbing* heart and *throngs* of camels. Echoing the same joy, the Gospel of Matthew tells us, "The sight of the star filled them with delight."

Epiphany means "manifestation." Is this misleading? The feast does not celebrate what God does but what we do: we *awaken* to the presence of God in our midst, symbolized by the Magi understanding the message and meaning of the star.

"We Three Kings" is a haunting song, but is it historical? The Magi who have captured our imagination down through the ages were not kings. There is no evidence of three figures or even any at all.

This matters little to those of us who live on the symbolic level. We don't make myths; myths make us. How impoverished would we be without the story of the Three Kings following the star and finding a treasure at the end of their journey?

The Journey

Epiphany celebrates the archetypal journey of all those who discover God because they search ardently. The story of the Magi is the story of our own journey. I love how German Jesuit Karl Rahner describes it:

> *Do we not all have to admit that we are pilgrims on a journey, who have no fixed abodes, even though we must never forget our native country? How time flies...how we are eternally in change, how we move from place to place. Somewhere, and at some time or other, we come into existence, and already have set out on the journey that goes on and on, and never again returns to the same place. The journey's path moves through childhood, through youthful strength, and through the maturity of age, through a few festal days and many routine weekdays. It moves through heights and misery, through purity and sin, through love and disillusion. On and on it goes, irresistibly on from the morning of life to the evening of death.*

Rahner says living means "passing through many levels of change... The [Magi's] way was long and their feet were often tired, their hearts often heavy and vexed.... But their hearts carry on to the end. They do not even know where the courage and strength keep coming from. It is not from themselves, and it simply suffices."

Strength and courage do not fail as long as we do not peer inquisitively into the empty reaches of our hearts to see if anything is inside. Strength and courage do not fail as long as

we bravely keep on spending, even squandering, the mysterious contents of our hearts. As St. Francis said, "It is in giving that we receive."

Epiphany as Archetype and Art

The Three Kings may never have existed, but their archetypal reality has dominated our human consciousness and therefore our art for over two thousand years.

I collect camel images and have several in my hermitage. I also have a vast collection of Three Kings Christmas cards. They express many Epiphany themes that reveal aspects of our own journey through life across dangerous archetypal terrain: rocky mountain passes, vast lonely deserts, storm-tossed seas. Are we traveling alone or in a full caravan? Is it dark? Are we afraid of ambush?

Most Christmas art shows the Magi's camels plodding along slowly, even stationary as they gaze at the star. But I have a card or two where the camels are running, symbolizing our own eagerness to arrive at our "destination." A special favorite is three shamans, three Native American Wise Men, riding horses through deep snow, clouds of breath condensing in the air.

I love the art portraying camels and kings in dark silhouette against bare trees, barren earth, or flaming red sunsets, often with the domed structures of Bethlehem in the distance. I love the more stylized versions in various shapes and colors, some cut out of paper. I love how often we see one of the kings pointing. Where? *To beyond themselves.* Sometimes the kings look more like simple shepherds. They wear no crowns and show humility enough to ask directions of those they meet along the way.

> A favorite Christmas card is three shamans, three Native American wise men, riding horses through deep snow, clouds of breath condensing in the air.

Another favorite image is from a piece of old stationery: in the foreground two of the Magi wave farewell to the third in the distance, going a separate way home. This also reminds me of "The Other Wise Man," Henry Van Dyke's story of a fourth wise man, Artaban (also a film starring Martin Sheen). Artaban sold all his possessions to buy three jewels to give to the mysterious Child. On his way to meet his other companions, he stops and uses one of the jewels to help a person in need. This keeps happening. He gives away all the jewels, never catches his comrades, and ends up as a beggar in the streets of Jerusalem. One day he sees a criminal being marched off to his execution. Arteban is sad he cannot help him, then learns "You've been helping me all your life."

Adoration of the Magi

Adoration is another prominent theme in my Christmas cards. When the Three Wise Men arrive at the stable, they fall to their knees and bow their heads before the Christ-Child. One offers gold: "I honor you as my King." The second offers frankincense: "I worship you as my God." The third offers myrrh: "I grieve over your death."

These depictions seem to be static, but are they? Adoration, or contemplation, may be interior and still, but it is active. Some call it the *highest* human act. G.K. Chesterton, probably a mystic himself, once said: "When we bow down in adoration, the whole world turns right side up." He also said: "If we cannot pray, we are gagged. If we cannot kneel, we are in chains."

> The Magi's gifts are strange from a child's point of view. The "Child just born" said, "I want the camel!"

Gift-giving at Christmas

Rahner maintains that the gift of gold symbolizes love, the frankincense reverence, and the myrrh suffering, both the Child's and our own. Through our own gift-giving at Christmas, we not only remember the Magi, we celebrate the mystery of the great Gift-Giver. The giving of gifts in an appropriate spirit, with no compulsion or competition, also symbolizes how we are called to give ourselves away. My favorite Christmas insight from Chesterton even describes material gift-giving as the essence of the feast of the Incarnation:

> *...she said that she did not give presents in a gross, sensuous, terrestrial sense, but sat still and thought about Truth and Purity till all her friends were much better for it. Now I do not say that this plan is either superstitious or impossible, and no doubt it has an economic charm. I say it is un-Christian... The idea of embodying goodwill—that is, of putting it into a body—is the huge and primal idea of the Incarnation. A gift of God that can be seen and touched is the whole point of the epigram of the creed. Christ Himself was*

a Christmas present. The note of material Christmas presents is struck even before He is born in the first movements of the sages and the star. The Three Kings came to Bethlehem bringing gold and frankincense and myrrh. If they had only brought Truth and Purity and Love there would have been no Christian art and no Christian civilization.

The Magi's gifts are strange from a child's point of view. Spanish poet Gloria Fuertes expressed what we all intuit when she wrote how astonished the men were to hear "a Child just born speak like a man" and say, "I want the camel, that's what I want!"

Amahl and the Night Visitors

Gian Carlo Menotti wrote his one-act opera, "Amahl and the Night Visitors," expressly for the Hallmark Hall of Fame on television in 1951. I watched it with my family year after year until 1966, when I graduated from college and it left the air.

Growing up in Italy, where children receive their gifts from the Three Kings, Menotti said he could "hear" them coming: "I remember the weird cadence of their song in the distance; I remember the brittle sound of the camel's hooves crushing the frozen snow; and I remember the mysterious tinkling of their silver bridles."

The opera has had a lasting impact on me. Amahl is a young crippled boy living in poverty alone with his mother. He has seen the unusually bright star earlier in the evening, but his mother doesn't believe him. Neither does she believe him when he tells her there's a king at the door; no, *two* kings; no, *three* kings at the door.

> Contemplation is still, but also active,
> perhaps the highest human act.

Old King Caspar is childlike, eccentric, and a bit deaf, keeping his treasures in a box: magic stones, beads, and licorice. Fifty years later, I can still hear this character singing "This is my box, this is my box, I never travel without my box." The tune is memorable, the words are memorable. But I've never forgotten this childhood Christmas experience because the box, or the treasure chest, is another archetypal image. What's in the box? What's in the chest? What *is* the treasure?

What's in the Box?

I even created a game out of this experience. Every Epiphany I get out an old cigar box and fill it with tiny gifts, one for each person present. We pass it around, everyone shakes it and smells it, trying to guess what's inside. Sometimes it takes a while, and sometimes the answer comes quickly. (I'll never forget the year Tom guessed "bath oil beads" on the first try!) You may want to play the game with your own children and friends after you bless your home with chalk, using the ritual which follows here.

The speeches of the Three Kings in the ritual are adapted from Menotti's opera. The C-M-B are the initials of the legendary names of the Magi. They originally stood for the first letters of the words in the Latin blessing, *Christus mansionem benedicat,* "May Christ bless this house." But the myth of the Three Kings claimed us instead.

A Ritual for Epiphany

Compiled by *Tessa Bielecki*

Gather holy water, incense, pieces of chalk, and "gold," such as chocolate coins. You often find frankincense and myrrh in Middle Eastern markets.

All Sing: We Three Kings of Orient are, bearing gifts we traverse afar. Field and fountain, moor and mountain, following yonder star.

Refrain: Oh, Star of wonder, star of night, star with royal beauty bright; Westward leading, still proceeding, guide us to thy perfect light.

First King: Have you seen a Child the color of wheat, the color of dawn? His eyes are mild, His hands are those of a King, as King He was born. Shining gold we bring to His side, and the Eastern Star is our Guide.

All Sing: Born a Babe on Bethlehem's plain; gold we bring to crown him again, King forever, ceasing never, over us all to reign. *(Refrain)*

Second King: Have you seen a Child the color of earth, the color of thorn? His eyes are sad, His hands are those of the poor, as poor He was born. Bitter myrrh we bring to His side, and the Eastern Star is our Guide.

All Sing: Myrrh is mine, its bitter perfume, breathes a life of gathering gloom; Sorrowing, sighing, bleeding, dying, sealed in a stone-cold tomb. *(Refrain)*

Third King: The Child we seek holds the seas and the winds on His palm. The Child we seek has the moon and the stars at His feet. Before Him the eagle is gentle and the lion is meek. Frankincense we bring to His side, and the Eastern Star is our Guide.

All Sing: Frankincense to offer have I, incense owns a deity nigh. Prayer and praising, all men raising, worshipping God on high. *(Refrain)*

All: The Child we seek has no need of gold. On love alone He builds His Kingdom. His pierced hand holds no scepter. His haloed head wears no crown. His might is not built on our toil. Swifter than lightning He now walks among us. The keys to His city belong to the poor. He takes away the sting of death and brings us new life. The gift of ourselves we bring to His side, and the Eastern Star is our Guide.

All Sing: Oh, star of wonder, star of night, star with royal beauty bright; Westward leading, still proceeding, guide us to thy perfect Light.

Following the Star

Leader: Wise men still seek him. We've all got to go chasing stars again. *(Frank Horne)*

Men: Look up, you there. Star-readers, this way! See, I am a new rising star. *(Rainer Maria Rilke)*

159

Women: Let my radiance into your existence. In this strong light, much will happen. (Rainer Maria Rilke)

Men: The star which they had seen in the East went before them, till it came to rest over the place where the Child was. When they saw the star, they rejoiced exceedingly. (Mt 2:9-11)

Women: To discover how to be human now/ Is the reason we follow the star. (W.H. Auden)

Men: I am the Root of Jesse and David's Son, the radiant star of morning, and God's own light. (Lucien Deiss)

Women: Because of the compassionate kindness of our God, the Daystar from on high will visit us, to shine on those who sit in darkness and the shadow of death. (Luke 1:79)

Men: I have seen the Morning Star, upon the distant horizon. All the shadows of the dark, cannot keep the sun from rising. (Tom Renaud)

Women: This world is wild as an old wives' tale, and strange the plain things are... Our peace is put in impossible things where clashed and thundered unthinkable wings round an incredible star. (G.K. Chesterton)

Men: To an open house in evening, home shall all men come... To the end of the way of the wandering star, to the things that cannot be and are, to the place where God was homeless, and all men are at home. (G.K. Chesterton)

Women: They saw a white star twinkle for a while. The beauty of it smote their hearts, and hope returned again.
(J.R.R. Tolkien)

Men: In the end, every Shadow is only a small passing thing. Beyond its dark reach, there is light and high beauty forever.
(J.R.R. Tolkien)

Women: The midst of the earth is a raging mirth and the heart of the earth a star. (G.K. Chesterton)

Leader: Wise men still seek him. We've all got to go chasing stars again. (Frank Horne)

Blessing
Gold, Frankincense, Myrrh, and Chalk

Leader: Our help is in the name of God, Our Creator.

All: Who made heaven and earth.

Leader: May the Holy Spirit be with you.

All: And also with you.

Leader: Let us pray. Accept O Creator, these gifts we humbly offer you. May you accept them as you once accepted the first fruits of the earth from Abel and gifts from the Three Magi.

All: Amen. Magi from the East came to Bethlehem to adore the Christ-Child; and opening their treasure chests, they presented him with precious gifts: gold for the great King, incense for the true God, and myrrh in symbol of his burial. Alleluia!

Leader: Let us pray. Oh invisible and endless One, be pleased to endow with your blessing and power these gifts of gold, incense, and myrrh. Protect those who have them in their possession from every kind of illness, injury, and danger, anything that would interfere with the well-being of body and soul, and enable them to live joyously and confidently in your Sacred Presence; You who live and reign forever and ever,

All: Amen.

(Leader blesses gifts with holy water and incenses them.)

Leader: Let us pray. Bless, O Creator, this chalk, and let it be a help to humanity. Grant that those who use it with trust in you and with it inscribe on the doors of their homes the names of your three Magi, Caspar, Melchior, and Balthasar, may through their merits and intercession enjoy health in body and protection of soul.

All: Amen. O God, who on this day revealed your son Jesus to all nations by the guidance of a star, grant that we who now know you by faith darkly may finally behold you in the light of your heavenly majesty. Amen. Alleluia! Alleluia!

(Leader blesses chalk with holy water and incense, then writes the initials of the Magi and the year on the lintel of the front door of the house, for example, like this: C 20 M 14 B.)

Men: Be enlightened and shine forth, O Jerusalem, for your light is come; and upon you is risen the glory of Jesus Christ, born of the Virgin Mary.

Women: Nations shall walk in your light, and kings in the splendor of your birth. The glory of God is risen upon you.

All: Alleluia! Alleluia!

16

Tracking the Magi

Who Were They?

Jasper Winn

As a child, my favorite carol was "We Three Kings." It had everything—a rousing tune and a stirring richness in the original words. It was a song that reeked of romance. Palm trees, dromedaries, bejewelled coronets, Arabian steeds with embroidered saddle cloths and, above all, journeying were suggested by the opening lines: "We Three Kings of Orient are, bearing gifts we travel afar."

As a small boy, it was an extra delight to discover that my own name came from one of the Magi. Delving into a dictionary of names as a nine-year-old, I read: "JASPER: Possibly Persian. Possible meanings: 'Treasure Bringer', 'Gold Keeper', 'The White King'. German: Casper. French: Gaspard. Spanish: Gaspar. In popular legend one of the Three Kings or Wise Men."

On foot of this reference I opened a Bible, perhaps for the first time of my own volition. It was a disappointing step backwards. The only reference to the Wise Men was in St.

Matthew's Gospel, and his account bore little relation to either the carol or the rich narrative of kindergarten theatrics. Matthew talked of an indeterminate number of Wise Men (not kings, and no names, camels, horses, or ornamented palanquins). And they were part of a rather macabre plot, coming to Jerusalem to find the prophesized newborn King of the Jews, meeting with Herod who redirected them to Bethlehem and being ordered by him to return with news of the child so that he, Herod, could "worship him also."

They found the holy child and presented him with gold, frankincense and myrrh (the only association with three of anything in the story). And then the Wise Men were warned by God in a dream not to return to Herod, and so made their way back to "their country" by another route.

Herod's reaction, "when he saw he was mocked of the Wise Men," was to order the death of all children of two years and under, "according to the time which he had diligently inquired of the Wise Men." This prompted the flight of the Holy Family into Egypt.

Marco Polo and the Magi's Tombs

At this point any feeling of a personal connection with the story of the journey of the Magi might have stalled for ever, had it not been jump-started by a visit to Iran many years later. There my name was recognised as that of one of the Three Kings, and the relevant pages of Marco Polo's travels put before me to show the connection. Suddenly I had the key to a greater understanding of the Nativity, the Epiphany and the significance of the Magi.

In Saveh, between Tehran and Qom in modern Iran, Marco Polo was said to have found the tombs of three Magi—their bodies uncorrupted, their hair and beards intact. He inquired about their story and was told that the three of them, one young, one middle-aged and one old, had set off from Saveh to find and worship a new-born prophet. They took with them gold, frankincense and myrrh. Which of these gifts the child chose would signify whether he was an earthly king, a god or a healer (shades in this of Tibetans offering significant relics to the child destined to be the Dalai Lama, the child's choice proving or disproving his status as the divine reincarnation).

Having found the child, each king entered his presence separately and alone, and each, in turn, encountered someone who was of their own age and appearance. But when they then went in all three together, they found a thirteen-day-old baby.

Fire in the Well

The child accepted the three gifts they offered, signifying he was an earthly king, a god and a healer. And in turn he gave the Magi a stone in a casket—a symbol of the constancy they should have in the faith they had now adopted by worshipping the newborn prophet.

> There are resonances with Zoroastrian worship of fire, which perhaps originated and was fueled by the ignitions of natural gas in oil-rich Central Asia.

Failing to realize its significance, they threw the stone into a well on their return journey. Immediately, a burning fire descended from heaven into the well. Repenting of their foolishness, they took some of the fire and carried it to Kala Atashparastan ("the town of the fire-worshippers"), some three days' travel from Saveh. From there the fire was passed on to other temples.

The neatness of this legend is exemplary. The Magi had been an independent seer caste for centuries before Christ's birth. As a priestly cult they held an arcane knowledge of magic (the word derives from the Greek transliteration of "Magi").

They also interpreted dreams and events for the Seleucids, Parthians and Sassanians, as well as for the Medes.

There is a further circling of events in the legend, for there are resonances with the Zoroastrian worship of fire (which perhaps originated and was fuelled by the ignitions of natural gas in oil-rich Central Asia). The Magi were connected with the early followers of Zoroaster, and according to a second-century apocryphal gospel sought the Christ-Child in fulfilment of a prophecy of Zoroaster himself.

> My mind filled with images of cara-
> vans plodding across vast sand dunes,
> of stallions draped in embroidered
> saddle cloths, of Damascus swords
> and silk turbans.

Adoration of the Magi

It follows that two thousand years ago, even though the caste had lost much of its influence (and had split into two groups, the Babylonian Magi who were seen as charlatans, and the Persian Magi, who retained their original powers and rituals), a new prophet, king and god would have to be vetted and accepted by the Magi. That there was a concordance between the beliefs of the Magi and what the birth of Christ foretold, must have helped that acceptance.

The Magi appear again and within a European context some time after the birth of Christ. The Priscilla Catacomb of Rome boasts the first extant depiction of the Adoration of the Magi, in a second-century fresco. In the eighth-century *Excerpta Latina Barberi,* the Magi are given names (though undoubtedly not for the first time)—Bithisarea, Melichior and Gathaspa. These became Balthasar, Melchior and Gaspar or

Casper in popular tradition, and they were represented as the kings of, respectively, Arabia, Persia and India.

In a further departure from the Iranian legend, the supposed relics of the Magi were held in Constantinople, from where, perhaps in the fifth century, they were transferred to Milan. From there they were moved, as pawns in a game of religious politics, to Cologne Cathedral in the twelfth century. At this period the Magi had become a rallying motif for the Crusades, and many representations of their story appear in the cathedrals of the time; rather charmingly, in Chartres one of a triptych of carved panels shows the Three Kings warmly tucked up in bed, crowns on, while one of them is told by an angel to avoid Herod on their return journey.

Patron Saints of Travellers

In medieval Europe the Magi became the patron saints of travellers. On learning this my mind filled again with images no different from those of my childhood—of caravans plodding across sand dunes, of stallions draped in embroidered saddle cloths, of Damascus swords, and silk turbans. But now they were all sights I had witnessed for myself since setting out on my own travels. And while journeying, I had learned perhaps every variation on my name; I had been called and answered to Gaspar, Yesper, Caspar, Gasparino, and Gaspard.

I had also rewritten the first line of my still favorite carol. "We indeterminate number of cultish seers, not really from the East but from out that way, carrying gifts we travel afar."

Interview with a Stargazer

Neyle Sollee, with David Denny

*Pathologist and astronomer Neyle Sollee used
to be my neighbor. When he lived in Colorado,
his observatory served him as a kind of oratory.
I asked him about astronomy and mathematics,
and how they affect his faith. Neyle's contribution
to our conversation follows.*

My interest in astronomy began in the early 1960s when I
wasn't following any serious religious path. I remember
reading in a little book about how we spend half our life under
the night sky. That struck me profoundly. I thought, "That's
right, and I don't know a thing about the night sky." I had never
studied astronomy. So I bought a little dollar book on the stars
and went out and looked through the trees and city lights of
Memphis. It took an hour to find the Big Dipper and I remember
how excited I was. I had never seen it before.

I was near graduation from dental school, but the interest
stayed with me on and off through the years. I was a member
of the Memphis Astronomical Society and had a little telescope
and an observatory in Memphis in 1980 before I moved out to
southern Colorado.

Throughout my life I was always looking through
microscopes or telescopes and cameras. These were never
separate endeavors. I was amazed: I couldn't resist the mystery

of it. I took some courses at night and read books. It resembled my discovery of mathematics.

When I was thirty-five years old I attended a pathology conference on laboratory instruments. A presenter showed us Maxwell's electrical magnetism equations. He said, "You guys out there probably don't know what these are. If you knew calculus you might understand that they are very beautiful." I remember the power of that and I said, "My Lord, they *are* beautiful. But I don't know anything about calculus." So I studied calculus for four or five years. I started on my math and science education and took undergraduate physics. That was my "math conversion." I was able to work for hours and hours and all weekend solving problems. It was an aesthetic conversion.

A Universe of Radiant Beauty

I finally realized after twenty years of study that I really was not a mathematician, but mathematicians confirmed my intuition that mathematics is elegant and beautiful. You would be surprised at the number of articles written on the beauty of physics.

The laws of the universe are embedded within us, and mathematics is the language God has used to describe the universe in some way. There is some mysterious thing about mathematics in the human being, because the laws that we know innately are the same laws that determine the physical workings of the universe. A great physicist wrote that the association between mathematics and nature is unreasonable. Well, to me it is obviously not unreasonable; it is how it should be, because the Creator creates.

When I look through time and space into the universe with my telescope, I am not looking at something alien. We know that we are made of stardust. That is not a romantic fantasy but good science. Physics, astrophysics, and math are not ultimately about building bombs or making toasters but about discovering and contemplating an intelligible universe of radiant beauty.

A Telescope Blessing

David Denny

Blessed are you, O Lord our God,
Creator of heaven and earth:
you created us in your image
and gave us hungry minds that feast on learning
and delight in exploring the wonders of your universe.

Bless this telescope,
an instrument for admiring the heavens
that proclaim your glory—
no speech, no word is heard,
yet their report goes forth through all the earth.
You know the number of the stars and call them by name.

Bless all who use this instrument.
May they be drawn to love the Mystery they approach
as they gaze through time and space
into the vast, majestic drama
of the birth, life, movement and death
of planets, stars, galaxies, and all celestial creatures.

Amen.

17

Scents of Time and Place

Harvesting Frankincense Today

Lark Ellen Gould

In the ancient world, particularly in the Middle East, beauty was as important as the air. It was in the gardens the people designed, the houses they built, the words they wrote, the very bowls they used, the candlesticks they carried, the fabrics they wove and the gifts they gave.

So when Christians ponder the gifts of the Magi as commemorated in the West during the feast of the Epiphany, the precious gold and fragrant frankincense and myrrh do not seem unusual for that time and place.

Gold, Frankincense, and Myrrh

What was unusual is that these gifts were presented to a child whose significance was yet to be understood.

St. Irenaeus, in his work *Adversus Haereses,* claimed the gifts were symbolic. Jesus was presented with gold for a king's wealth, frankincense as the fragrance offered to divinity and myrrh as the balm used to anoint the dead.

Although the identity of the Magi remains a mystery (they have been variously described as wise men, kings, priests or magicians), we know for certain that firmly established trade routes enabled the travelers to bring their offerings from remote areas to Palestine. The three gifts, including gold that in today's market would cost about $325 per ounce, would have been a kingly offering.

Scented Silk Tassels

Scents were believed to bring good will and good wishes. Frankincense and myrrh were used to perfume ceremonial oils. When burned, the smoke was thought to bring prayers to the heavens. Even today, during liturgies of the Eastern and Western churches, incense is often burned.

In the Arab world, the scenting of guests is a gesture that has been in practice for more than one thousand years. Scents stimulate the senses. The silk of cotton tassels of the *dishdashas* worn by the men of the Gulf are sewn into the garment for this reason. The perfume on the tassels lasts all day and serves as a gentle greeting as men welcome each other by offering their tassels to smell.

The Bible has no shortage of references to frankincense and myrrh resins cultivated from desert-growing trees. Oils scented with them are noted nearly two hundred times.

When God spoke to Moses on Mount Sinai he prescribed that a sacred ointment should contain quantities of pure myrrh and perfume or incense should contain quantities of frankincense. The use of frankincense by the Jews is noted in the Pentateuch as an ingredient to be used with the bread of the Sabbath and stored with other valued spices in the great chamber of the temple at Jerusalem.

Following the crucifixion, Nicodemus brought a mixture of myrrh and aloes for the linen shroud of Jesus. Indeed, the crown of thorns that Christ wore on the cross may have been formed from the sharp claws of the myrrh bush.

The Ancient Frankincense Trail

Oman was the starting point for the frankincense trail that took the fragrant gums from what are Oman, Yemen and

Somalia today and sent them up the Red Sea to Egypt and throughout the reaches of the Roman Empire. The gums that bubble from the trees into pearly white beads can still be found in southern Oman. Herodotus wrote that more than two tons were burned annually in the Temple of Baal in Babylon. Darius, King of Persia, received some twenty-five tons of incense every year. Nero was a great lover of the scent and burned a year's worth of the crop at the funeral of his wife, Poppaea.

The Egyptians embalmed their kings with frankincense and considered the fruit of the *Boswellia* or frankincense tree the perfume of the gods that, when collected and preserved correctly, ensured immortality. Pliny noted how control of the frankincense trade had made the southern Arabians the richest people in the world. It was said the trees were so valuable that snakes guarded them.

White Tears of Aromatic Amber

Today, in Oman's southernmost region of Dhofar, which borders Saudi Arabia's vast and empty Rub al-Khali desert to the north and west and the upper curve of southern Yemen to the south, the stubby, thorny trees live where little else will. The trees can only grow when a complex set of conditions has been met: limestone soil and a climate with high humidity in a desert that receives little rain.

In Oman, frankincense accounted for three-quarters of the country's gross national product until the bottom fell out of what was once a thriving trade. The finest grades of frankincense are still used for high-end perfume manufacturing. But gums of all grades can be found in the local *souqs,* especially "frankincense alley" in the country's southern port of Salalah and the perfume market at Mutrah Souq in Oman's capital, Muscat. The people who buy are local, burning it for its antiseptic purposes, perfuming hair with the smoke, chewing it for digestion.

The frankincense trees release the aromatic amber for only a few weeks in late summer. Gathering the resin has been a family-run business for centuries. Then, as now, the harvesting skill has been passed from father to son.

Musallem Rehaba, sixty-one, moves through a grove of trees that his family has owned for more than two hundred years—although the trees are much older—hacking at the bark with a *mangis* or chafing tool. Although it is March, and nowhere near harvesting season, white tears bead up along the newly exposed bark but do not make enough of a globule to collect in the tin bucket he has placed by its roots.

The area is strewn with empty bottles and bleached bones, remnants of picnics from last summer when the family spent days collecting resin on the wind-swept hill. Rehaba's sons help him, but they will not take over the trade when their father dies.

"Harvests are better than when I was little and watched my father work with the trees," said Rehaba. "Even though we are Bedouins we have a house and many camels and this work is very hard. We did this because it was our tradition. But money? Nothing much. I do not know what will happen to the trees."

"Only the people who live around them can touch them. It is easy to ruin a tree. You have to know where to cut," he said. As he goes about making cuts, he sings a song about the frankincense trees that his father used to sing when he was harvesting them.

Omani frankincense is top grade—pure and very rare—and accounts for about ten percent of the six hundred tons that are harvested worldwide each year. And it is expensive—about double what other grades cost.

As in biblical times, when the magi offered the most valuable essences known to man, the practice continues. When presented in a gold coffer, the gift of hard-hewn pearls of frankincense and myrrh remains precious.

If, as Herod
we fill our lives with things,
and again with things;
if we consider ourselves
so unimportant that
we must fill every moment of
our lives with action,
when will we have the time to
make the long slow journey
across the desert as did the
Magi?
Or sit and watch the stars as
did the shepherds?
Or brood over the coming of
the child as did Mary?
For each one of us there is a
desert to cross, a star to discover, and a
being within ourselves to bring to life.

Author Unknown

Part 6
Candlemas

Light the candles.
They have more right to exist than all the darkness.
It is Christmas, Christmas that lasts forever.

Karl Rahner, S.J.

It don't take a lot of money
to know what riches are,
Just a candle in the window
and Christmas in your heart.
Alabama

Candlemas, celebrated on February 2, is the

fortieth day after the birth of Jesus and the traditional conclusion of the Christmas season. This feast is also known as the Presentation, when Mary and Joseph visited the Temple to "present" Jesus to God.

Celebrate this feast with a candle blessing. Find out how hollyhocks came to New Mexico and why Fr. Dave calls himself "David of the Presentation." And remember that after the Presentation, the Holy Family fled into Egypt to escape the wrath of King Herod.

One of my favorite Christmas cards is part of a painting, "Rest on the Flight into Egypt," created in 1879 by French artist Luc Olivier Merson. Mary and Jesus sleep between the "paws" of the Sphinx, light gleaming above the Christ-Child, sand from the desert piled at the base of the massive sculpture as Mary's leg dangles over the edge.

In the foreground of the original work, the faithful donkey, who has carried mother and child so far into a foreign land, forages on meager desert grasses. By a smoldering camp fire, Joseph stretches out and sleeps in the sand, exhausted. In the early twentieth century, Agnes Repplier from Philadelphia described the painting beautifully in her poem, "Le Repos en Egypte: The Sphinx," preparing us for the final days of the Christmas season:

> *All day I watch the stretch of burning sand;*
> *All night I brood beneath the golden stars...*
> *Built by the proudest of a kingly line,*
> *Over my head the centuries fly fast;*
> *The secrets of the mighty dead are mine;*
> *I hold the key of a forgotten past.*
> *Yet, ever hushed into a rapturous dream,*
> *I see again that night. A halo mild*
> *Shone from the liquid moon. Beneath her beam*
> *Traveled a tired young Mother and the Child.*
> *Within mine arms she slumbered, and alone*
> *I watched the Infant. At my feet her guide*
> *Lay stretched o'er-wearied. On my breast of stone*
> *Rested the Crucified.*

—*Tessa Bielecki*

I wish you, at this season,
peace as deep as a winter night
and joy as brave as a candle—
one candle in the deepest dark,
from which innumerable candles
can be lit to brighten our world.

David Steindl-Rast, O.S.B.

179

Glad Tidings for Candlemas

God's glory, now, is kindled gentler
than low candlelight
under the rafters of a barn:
Eternal Peace is sleeping in the hay,
and Wisdom's born in secret
in a straw-roofed stable.
Thomas Merton

A candle loses nothing of its light when lighting another.
Kahlil Gibran

It's better to light one candle than to curse the darkness.
Chinese Proverb

Who will kneel them gently down before the Lord newborn?...
many children, God give them grace,
bringing tall candles to light Mary's face.
Old Spanish Carol

Wherever the years may take me
no matter how far I go,
There's going to be a candle burning,
it's always nice to know.
Alabama

Some candle clear burns somewhere I come by.
I muse at how its being puts blissful back
With yellowy moisture mild night's blear-all black,
Or to-fro tender trambeams truckle at the eye.
Gerard Manley Hopkins

18

Mother of Candlelight and Sorrow

Befriending the Night

David Denny

I grew up in a Protestant family, so I learned about Roman Catholic feast days when I was in college and began making retreats in Sedona, Arizona. I discovered the feasts that followed Christmas and loved the reading from Isaiah that accompanied the Epiphany Mass. With its references to dromedaries and frankincense, it reminded me of my student adventures in the Middle East.

Forty Days of Christmas

I found out that in the "old days," the Christmas season extended for forty days, like Lent. It ended on February 2, the

Feast of the Presentation or Candlemas. This feast commemorates Mary and Joseph's visit to the Temple to "present" Jesus to God. Here we meet Simeon and Anna, elders who sense unprecedented holiness in the young couple's infant.

February 2 is also a pre-Christian holy day. In Ireland, it marked the first day of spring. Christmas, Epiphany, the Feast of Christ's Baptism, and Candlemas all celebrate Jesus as the Light of the world triumphing over the darkness of winter. It is customary to bless candles on this day, commemorating a final epiphany before the resumption of "ordinary time." And it was around this day that I entered monastic life in 1975.

> In the "old days," the Christmas season extended for forty days like Lent, and ended on February 2, the Feast of the Presentation or Candlemas.

Confusing Solace

One of my first memories of Roman Catholic worship was Mass in the monastery's half-underground chapel in Sedona. Its narrow faceted stained glass windows illuminated a simple wooden tabernacle adorned with a wrought iron cross. The reds and blues of the windows spilled onto the plush white carpet. The slump block walls were bare, except for small sconces for reading at night. Between liturgies, the portable altar disappeared, as did all other furniture.

Monks and guests sat on the carpet and leaned against the cool walls. It smelled like frankincense and bees' wax. This kiva-like quality spoke to me deeply. Having lived briefly with families in Afghanistan and Mexico, I suffered anxiety and insomnia in suburban Arizona's air-conditioned and malled divorce from the desert's raw beauty. I found solace lying down under the stars or descending barefoot into the chapel.

I found a confusing kind of solace when I attended Mass in parishes beyond the monastery. I didn't trust this consolation that arose out of a sense of "tackiness" that was new to me. The Protestant churches I had attended were restrained. Now for the first time, I was exposed to the "garish" statues, plastic flowers, and unfamiliar devotions of Mexican-American Catholicism.

Earthy Southwestern Art

I keep discovering more about the deep spirit and artistry of the people who have inhabited the American Southwest for centuries. Gradually, over forty years in the Southwest, I exchanged my air-conditioned suburban isolation from the native environment for something earthier, more "primitive." It took a while, partly because I was so focused on learning about monastic history and practice. I zealously absorbed the spirit of European Catholicism and the Carmelite tradition.

But after thirty years, I left monastic life and found myself in a new context, as a teacher, writer and priest falling in love again with the physical desert and the desert spirit of the artists and arts of Spanish colonial New Mexico and Colorado.

A common thread, from then until now, is my love for Candlemas, the Feast of the Presentation, and a gradually deepening devotion to Mary, not through European apparitions at Lourdes or Fatima, but through Dante's *Divine Comedy* and Our Lady of Sorrows and Our Lady of Solitude as represented in *retablos* and *bultos* (statues) in the Spanish colonial style.

David of the Presentation

When I entered monastic life, I took the name David of the Presentation. It appealed to me because the Presentation was a "family" feast: Joseph and Mary bring the Child Jesus to the Temple in Jerusalem. It also appealed to me because of the mysterious Simeon, who intuited that this infant was "destined for the fall and rise of many in Israel, and to be a sign that will be contradicted." Why must something so good and beautiful provoke so much unrest and resistance?

To this scriptural association of Mary with light and sorrow, glory and a pierced heart, was added the Blessed Virgin's association with evening and night. Monks recite or sing Mary's *Magnificat*, Simeon's *Nunc dimittis*, and the hymn *Salve Regina* at Vespers and Compline.

I learned that the "night" was St. John of the Cross' central poetic metaphor for harrowing and divinizing growth. For John, it is a "happy night" because it unites us with our Beloved. It is the "night truly blessed" proclaimed at the Easter Vigil, "when heaven is wedded to earth" and we are reconciled to God. I sensed that under the *Shekina*-like canopy of Mary's maternal presence, we need not "fear the terror of the night... nor the plague that prowls in the darkness."

As a child I suffered nightmares, and this pairing of night and maternal protection touched a vulnerable spot in me. But John's erotic imagery echoed the Song of Songs, and gave me some intuition that despite the difficulties of celibacy, this solitary commitment need not be sterile but life-giving.

Queen of Everlasting Day

Years after discovering St. John of the Cross I discovered Dante, who introduced me to Mary's association with light. At the beginning of *Purgatory*, we meet the "Negligent Rulers" who sing the *Salve Regina* as daylight fades. But the Blessed Virgin of Dante's *Paradise* is Queen of everlasting day. And although I am awed by Mary "the lovely sapphire / whose grace ensapphires the heaven's brightest sphere" and whose presence makes heaven "more divine," at this point in my life, I have a deeper devotion to the earthbound New Mexican images of the Mother of Sorrows.

In the nineteenth century, holy men in Northern New Mexico carved images of the Virgin with her heart pierced by seven swords, or standing alone as Our Lady of Solitude, a crone whose power comes not from exaltation in heaven, but from earthly loss. *Nuestra Señora de la Soledad* is a woman who has lost child and husband, who has endured the "Seven Sorrows" that began with Simeon's premonition and ended with Jesus' excommunication and death.

A few years ago in Santa Fe I offered a seminar on grief in which we read poems of faith and despair. As poets voiced the fears, anger, and sense of groundlessness that death and loss inflame, we shared our own sorrows.

> The mysterious Simeon intuited that Jesus was destined to be a sign of contradiction. Why must something so good provoke so much resistance?

One day we visited the home studio of Arlene Cisneros-Sena, a contemporary *santera* who painted the St. Joseph *reredos* in the Santa Fe Basilica's Blessed Sacrament chapel. Her home is populated with scores of *santos,* both paintings and statues depicting the lives of Jesus, Mary and the favorite saints of New Mexico. These are not objets d'art but presences. According to Thomas Steele, Jesuit collector of *santos*, these images *participate* in the life and love of the saints they represent. Arlene's house is full of light and color radiating from these sacred images.

Many of the pigments derive from native minerals, vegetables, and even insects that burrow beneath the skin of prickly pear cactus. The paintings are varnished with sap from piñon pines that flourish in arid New Mexico.

Yes, we saw images of the Mother of Sorrows and Our Lady of Solitude and Christ Crucified. But the atmosphere surrounding these images gave us strength and hope because they mediated the living presence of the communion of saints.

I look to the rough-hewn Mary who fashions tortillas and listens to her children's banter and woes, a woman with a broken heart and a candle in her hand on a dark February night.

As I look back on my life in the Church and my devotion to the Feast of the Presentation, I find myself looking not so much to Dante's celestial Virgin, but to the unrefined *retablos* and *bultos* of the churches of Chimayó and Ranchos de Taos, New Mexico. Not the Mystical Rose in the undying day of Paradise, but the rough-hewn figure who fashions tortillas and listens to her children's banter and woes, anxieties and dreams.

Philosophers and theologians are not much help to me when tragedy strikes. I need a friend. I need the earth. I need, as the Aztecs knew, flower and song, *flor y canto*. I need, not a woman clothed with the sun, but a woman with a broken heart and a candle in her hand on a dark February night.

186

Simeon

David Denny

I would give away my life
For a burden lighter than the one I carry,
The unwieldy one that claims my name.
A man is never old in years,
But this load has been old and heavy
All my life.
I am looking for a new burden
That doesn't crush the earth or block
The paths of spinning dancers: someone
I could hold in my own two arms,
a child, a child strong enough
To bear the weight of all the tears
That ever fell,
Of all the lies we ever told;
Someone who would make me laugh
Over and over like a child
Or like a wise and holy man
Who spies death galloping nearer.

A Candlemas Blessing

Compiled by Tessa Bielecki

Leader: Light the candles! They have more right to exist than all the darkness. *(Karl Rahner, S.J.)*

All: Candles of joy, despite all sadness,
Candles of hope, where despair keeps watch,
Candles of courage for fears ever present,
Candles of peace for tempest-tossed days,
Candles of grace to ease heavy burdens,
Candles of love to inspire all our living,
Candles to burn the year long. *(Howard Thurman)*

Leader: Maker of the Universe, Source of All Light, Spirit of All That Is, bless these candles. *(Sprinkle candles with holy water and incense them.)* May we who use them to bring light out of darkness come with joy to the Light that shines forever.

All: Amen. May these candles light our way through the dark until the dawn comes and the morning star rises in our hearts.

Reader: *A Reading from the Prophet Isaiah*

The people that walked in darkness has seen a great light; on those who live in a land of deep shadow a light has shone. You have made their gladness greater, you have made their joy increase; they rejoice in your presence as they rejoice at harvest time.... Rise up in splendor, your light has come. No more shall the sun be your light by day, nor the moon enlighten you by night. The Lord God shall be your everlasting light, and you shall be radiant at what you see.

All: I have seen the Morning Star, upon the distant horizon. All the shadows of the dark, cannot keep the sun from rising. *(Tom Renaud)*

Christ for All People

Celebrating a World of Christian Art

Ron O'Grady, editor

New York: Orbis Books, 2001

Reflection by David Denny

If, like mine, your life is too "wordy," feast your eyes on this full-color collection of contemporary Christian art from around the world. Or if you tend to read the Gospel in what the late theologian Frank Sheed called a "pious coma," then this book will be salubriously startling.

After a quick summary of the history of Christian art, *Christ for All People* guides the reader and viewer through an illustrated life of Christ. We meet Sri Lankan Magi who look like red-cheeked children dressed in wild indigo and red robes under a fireworks display. The next image of Magi, by Agha Behzad, is a twentieth-century Persian miniature. Instead of the Wise Men from afar, these Magi are locals coming to honor one of their own.

> A white Persian donkey has a clear sense of hierarchy: he is indoors and Mary is outside. Joseph looks puzzled.

My own strange tastes lead me to watch for donkey depictions, and this trove contains many. But none as noble as Behzad's white Persian donkey with a clear sense of hierarchy: he's indoors and Mary is outside. Joseph looks puzzled by this unusual arrangement.

Nigerian Annunciation

Images of Mary are wide-ranging. Woelfel's *Nigerian Annunciation* is a simple stippled two-dimensional work with Mary looking like a breathtaking hip-hop diva. Before her kneels the angel Gabriel, delicately wielding what may be wooden tweezers that hold a white envelope containing the wildest invitation ever delivered. *Mother of God of Chernobyl* and the *Stalingrad Madonna* are full of pathos. The stories behind some of the images are heartbreaking. Kurt Reuber, who sketched the *Stalingrad Madonna* on the back of a military map on Christmas 1942, was an artist, a priest, and a doctor. He died in a Russian prison camp the following winter.

> Jesus stands out because of his white sleeveless t-shirt, black beard, and canary-rimmed sunglasses. The motley disciples are gangly and barefoot.

Depictions of Christ have ranged from formal and otherworldly to natural and human. Hany Sameer's *Holy Family on the River Nile* is a warm balance of these two poles. While it includes the gold leaf and somewhat stylized forms of the Coptic and Byzantine traditions, the yellow-orange halo around the Holy Family exudes unusual warmth, as does the presence of a dog, whose head hangs over the gunwale, gazing down at a submerged reflection of an Egyptian god, receding beneath the baptismal waters of the New Moses.

Reggae Rabbi

On the radically human end of the scale lies Indonesian Bagong Kussudiardja's *Christ and the Fishermen*. These guys remind me of fishermen I met years ago in northeastern Brazil. Jesus stands out because of his white sleeveless t-shirt, black beard, and canary-rimmed sunglasses. The men are gangly and barefoot, and at first it seems way too casual. But then I remembered how in Brazil and other developing countries, the poor wear the cast-off clothing of the wealthy. So they look hip and stylish at first, until you notice the rips and patches. I would love to do some drumming with these motley apostles and their reggae rabbi!

Christ in Chicago

The Entry of Christ into Chicago in 1976, by American Roger Brown, portrays a stark contrast to the Indonesian beach. While most of Chicago's citizens, many of them black silhouettes in illuminated high-rises, ignore what's happening on the street, a flatbed truck rolls slowly up a main artery, with white-robed Jesus waving like a lonely celebrity to a few people along the sidewalk. One figure places a palm frond on the street and a bishop, two guitarists, and five politicians await Christ's arrival from a grandstand draped in red, white and blue bunting.

Turn the page, and the Windy City's faceless figures dwarfed by glass, stone, and pre-stressed concrete are replaced by warm colors and large almond-shaped Ethiopian eyes gazing in amazement and grief at the humble God-man.

Resurrection from a Fiery Abyss

An Australian Last Supper glitters with suspense and pathos as friends look to their doomed leader in candlelight that ought to be warm, but gives only unsettling, heatless light. Two mysterious angelic profiles weep in the dark periphery.

A Taiwanese Crucifixion depicts the cross as twigs; Jesus, like the insect we used to call a walking stick, blends with the twig, a reed bruised past recognition and combustible as tinder.

For me, the most heartrending juxtaposition of words and image appears on pages 146–147. A poem by Korea's Kwok Pui-lan faces a Crucifixion by He Qi of China. Get this book if only to read and see this last judgment in shantytown.

But Resurrection is the ultimate truth, and Andre Kamba Luesa's *Resurrection* glows with joy and music, laughter and triumph, as Christ rises from a fiery abyss, dressed in the splendid print clothing of Zaire and the Congo.

How Hollyhocks Came to New Mexico

Rudolfo Anaya

Los Ranchos, New Mexico: Rio Grande
Books, 2012

Reflection by Tessa Bielecki

The Three Kings have come and gone. King Herod has sent out his henchmen to slaughter every male infant in Bethlehem. Joseph is warned in a dream to take Mary and Jesus and flee into Egypt.

There's no trusty donkey in this version of the tale. Instead, an angel named *Sueño*, "sleep" or "dream" in Spanish, carries the Holy Family on his back. Because he's near-sighted as well as asleep, a charming detail, he thinks the Rio Grande is the Nile and drops the family off in New Mexico.

Mary learns how to make blue corn tortillas. Jesus gathers piñon nuts and comes to love green chile peppers. Joseph helps the pueblo people make ladders for their ceremonial kivas.

The family has many adventures in Belén, Chimayó, and at native dances, where the people lay green pine boughs and ears of corn at Jesus' feet. And eventually the family finds the way home.

The book is beautifully illustrated by Nicolás Otero, a *santero*, or artist who depicts saints, who modeled his drawings after traditional New Mexican *retablos*.

The hollyhocks in Anaya's own backyard inspired him to write the story. "The hollyhock may not have appeared in folktales," he says, "but it's part of us. It's the poor family's flower. Hollyhocks are so beautiful, they require so little care, and they bloom and bloom most of the summer…against every wall in New Mexico."

Where did hollyhocks come from? Read the story to find the answer from Anaya, New Mexico's master storyteller.

Verse for a Christmas Card

Helen Condon, R.S.C.J.

Today would they have come in a borrowed car
bumper to bumper, looking for a place
"No Vacancy" on all the motels?
Would the birthing be in a gas station
passersby, homeless too, offering help?
Beyond the DJ music could they hear
a new song piercing the night
stars dancing, and a child's first cry?

Star Thistle

David Denny

The camels get a lot of credit:
A cold coming they had
And pounding heat. But they came and they went.

   Me, I sometimes stop and stare
   At a star no longer there.

I haven't traveled much
Since that run to the Nile.
And after, he didn't stray far from the shop

Until he fled to the dust
And came back lean and restless.
I took him to towns, the hills, the lake.

He loved figs and knew
That I love thistle buds.
He liked to tease me, so he'd say

"I remember you when you
Were nothing but rabbit ears
And rickety stick-legs." (Of course

He didn't know me then;
I remember him in diapers.)
He never struck me; he cleaned my hooves.

After what they did
To him I wanted to die.
But that's the good thing about

Being asinine:

    Yes, I sometimes stop
    And stare at a star no longer there

And these days I'm dumb enough
To see starlight in
A thistle blossom and I eat it.

I may walk on, or stop
And stare at a stalk and taste
A star on my tongue, like honey or fig.

May that Holy Star
Grow every year more bright,
And send its glorious beam afar
To fill the world with light.

William Cullen Bryant

To a New Moses

David Denny

These are your people and this your land,
    If only for a while.
Our inn is a desert—we've plenty of room
    And water from the Nile.
Take refuge here from Herod's hand.
    Oh what a blessed day!
Here in our tent, here by the fire
    Our Savior came to stay.

*Painted on a small sheet of gold-fibered papyrus, the Arabic
caption for the image above announces "the entry of Our Lord
into Egypt with his mother and Joseph the carpenter." Egyptian
Coptic Christians trace their origins to St. Mark the Evangelist
and have a lively devotion to the Holy Family, who found shelter
in Egypt during Jesus' infancy.*

I will honor Christmas in my heart,
and try to keep it all the year.

Charles Dickens

W hen the song of the angels is stilled,
when the star in the sky is gone,
when the shepherds are back with their flocks,
the work of Christmas begins:
    to find the lost, to heal the broken,
    to feed the hungry, to release the prisoner,
    to rebuild the nations, to bring peace among all,
    to make music in the heart.

Howard Thurman

About the Authors

Tessa Bielecki and Fr. David Denny have worked together for over forty years. They began as Carmelite monks in the Spiritual Life Institute where they co-edited *Desert Call* and gave retreats and workshops. At Colorado College they taught a history of Christian Mysticism and *Desert Spirituality: from the Middle East to the American Southwest*. They left monastic life in 2005 and created the Desert Foundation (see www.desertfound.org) and now live in neighboring hermitages near Crestone, Colorado. Tessa is the author of three books on St. Teresa of Avila and recorded *Wild at Heart: Radical Teachings of the Christian Mystics* for Sounds True. Fr. Dave has served as chaplain for *Image* Journal's Glen Workshops and Seattle Pacific University's writing residencies. He raises funds for Cross Catholic Outreach, a relief ministry for the poorest of the poor. Both authors are currently working on their memoirs and collaborating again on *Fire and Light: the Passion of the Christian Mystics*.

Notes

Back Cover

You will find more information on *A Family Christmas* by Caroline Kennedy on page 85.

Introduction

iii Art by Deborah Dyer, an artist who lives in Newton, Massachusetts. Deborah also did the art on pages 5, 21 and 27, 45, 56, 98, 117, and 128.

Part 1: Advent

1 © Can Stock Photo Inc./Krisdog

2 © Can Stock Photo Inc./gmborden. The music ball also appears on pages 46, 60, 118, 148, 178, 197 and 199.

4 © Can Stock Photo Inc./agrino

9 © Can Stock Photo Inc./VladoV

10 © Can Stock Photo Inc./Daria

11 Dorothy McFarland lived somewhere in Massachusetts when she gave us this poem in 1978. The Greek word *metanoeite* is usually translated "Repent," but a more accurate meaning is "Convert" or "Change your ways."

13 Artist unknown. For almost fifty years, Tessa has clipped Christmas art and quotations from greeting cards, church bulletins and newsletters from friends, never expecting to publish any of them. It has been impossible to find all the original sources. If you know any, please contact us so we can give proper credit in future printings.

17 Sharon Doyle, former prioress of the Spiritual Life Institute, now lives in Wolfville, Nova Scotia. She is an adjunct professor at Acadia University and also serves as counsellor and offers spiritual accompaniment for the L'Arche Homefires community.

17, 20 Terry Sullivan Prevéy was also a member of the Spiritual Life Institute when she illustrated the Alfred Delp passage for an Advent greeting in the early 1970s. She also drew the pregnant Mary on page 42 and Simeon on page 187 for other Advent cards around the same time. Terry is now Office Management Specialist for the Deputy Chief of Mission, U.S. Embassy, Montevideo, Uruguay.

30 Decades ago, David Denny drew this stag to illustrate his *Christian Bestiary* when it first appeared in *Desert Call*. He also drew the art on pages 78 and 87.

39 "Don't stop the party" by Melanie McDonagh was originally published in *The Tablet*, 4 January 2003, and is reproduced here with permission of the Publisher. Visit http://www.thetablet.co.uk.

42 The quotation from John Lynch here and other passages elsewhere in this book, especially in "The Mysticism of Motherhood," are taken from Lynch's classic epic poem, *Woman Wrapped in Silence*, published by Paulist Press, Mahwah, New Jersey.

Part 2: Winter

47 Robert Rose lives in Wolfville, Nova Scotia where he serves as an assistant at L'Arche Homefires community. He also spent time at the Spiritual Life Institute.

48 © Can Stock Photo Inc./agrino. The snowflake repeats on page 57.

49 © Can Stock Photo Inc./jstan

53 Artist unknown

57 Annie Dillard, *Pilgrim at Tinker Creek* (New York: HarperCollins, 1974)

Part 3: Christmas

59 © Can Stock Photo Inc./huhulin

63 http://books.simonandschuster.com/Christmas-Carol-(Reissue)/Charles-Dickens/9780743563802

64-65 © Can Stock Photo Inc./yupiramos. The manger repeats on pages 62 and 115. The star repeats on pages 150, 159, 175, and 195. The camel appears on page 156 and the Wise Man on page 167.

67 © Can Stock Photo Inc./prawny

70 © Can Stock Photo Inc./kudryaska

75-77 Art and bi-lingual translation by Larry Torres. At LarTor.com you can purchase the full translation of *Las Posadas* and other writings, including *Folk Dramas for the Advent Season* and *The Four Apparitions of Guadalupe.*

79 Celtic artist unknown

87 Peter Beagle, *The Last Unicorn* (New York: Ballantine Books, 1968); Anne Morrow Lindbergh, *The Unicorn and Other Poems (1935-1955)* (Vintage Books, 1972)

97 Artist unknown

99 Frank Horne wrote this poem in December of 1942. It has been republished in many books and magazines and all over the internet.

102 Letter to the *London Times* is taken from Caroline

Kennedy's *A Family Christmas.*

103 Elinor Bowen, an artist living in Denver, Colorado, drew this "Elemental Christ" specifically to illustrate David Denny's article when it first appeared in *Desert Call.*

106 David Denny took this photo of the fish fossil, which was given to him by Carol and David Crawford, neighbors and friends in Crestone.

109, 111 © Can Stock Photo Inc./Pimonova

Part 4: The New Year

117 Several years ago, Bro. David Steindl-Rast, O.S.B. sent this angel greeting to us and many of his other friends. He also sent us the greeting on page 179.

120 © Can Stock Inc./agrino. The bell also appears on pages 124 and 145.

121 Art by Leslie McNamara, an artist from Santa Fe, New Mexico, who has been our friend for almost fifty years

125 Artist unknown

133 Tessa Bielecki calls the classical New Mexican "Story Teller" sculpture the "Mother of Millions." David Denny took this photo of Tessa's "Story Teller" and "posterized" it, along with his mesa photo on page 134.

144 © Can Stock Photo Inc./agrino. The tree also appears on pages i and 198.

Part 5: Epiphany

147 © Can Stock Photo Inc./alvaroc

149 Fr. Bede Griffiths, an English Benedictine monk, inspired Shantivanam Ashram in Kulittali, southern India for many years before his death in 1993. This insight

is from one of his sermons for the Twelve Days of Christmas.

151 © Can Stock Photo Inc./kirstypargeter

153 David Denny "posterized" these Three Kings cards from Tessa Bielecki's collection as well as the adoration image on page 162.

156 You will find recordings and films of *Amahl and the Night Visitors* on the internet. You may be especially interested in a short YouTube clip of the Three Kings singing "Do You Know a Child," adapted for your use here in Tessa's ritual for Epiphany.

158 © Can Stock Photo Inc./ArenaPhoto

163 "Tracking the Magi" by Jasper Winn was published in *The Tablet,* 2 January 1999, and is reproduced here with permission of the Publisher. Visit http://www.thetablet. co.uk. © Can Stock Photo Inc./#497579

168 Photo compliments of Neyle Sollee, M.D. from Memphis, Tennessee

170 Large stars by Deborah Dyer and star "shower" by David Denny

171, 174 David Denny took this photo of his ceramic camel plate made in Palestine. Lark Ellen Gould writes about Middle Eastern culture and arts. This article first appeared in the January-February 2003 issue of *CNEWA World* and is reprinted with permission. The bimonthly magazine of the Catholic Near East Welfare Association is now called *One*. See www.cnewa.org for information.

Part 6: Candlemas

177 © Can Stock Photo Inc./Dimanchik

180 © Can Stock Photo Inc./agrino. The candle also appears on page 188.

181 David Denny "posterized" his photo of this terra cotta statue of Our Lady of Guadalupe, a gift to Tessa from Cynthia West.

186 © Can Stock Photo Inc./PhotoHS

188 Howard Thurman's candle prayer and the quotation on page 197 are found in many sources at Christmastime. We tracked them down in Thurman's *Mood of Christmas and Other Celebrations* (Richmond, Indiana: Friends United Press, 2011.) The candle prayer has also been set to music.

193 Sister Helen Condon, now deceased, taught English at Barat College in Lake Forest, Illinois. This poem originally appeared in *RSCJ: A Journal of Reflection*, Summer/Fall 1989. (The journal is no longer published.) The gas station image originally appeared in www.experiencingla.com, adapted and "posterized" by David Denny. He also did the star "shower."

194 Leslie McNamara painted this donkey watercolor as her Christmas greeting for us several years ago. Tessa asked Fr. Dave to write a poem inspired by the art.

196 David Denny found this papyrus of the Holy Family on his trip to Egypt in 2005. It now hangs in his hermitage in Crestone.

Colophon

The main text of Season of Glad Songs *is set in Times New Roman typeface. Poetry and certain heads are set in Adobe Garamond Pro. Chapter and article titles are set in Balzano Standard.*

Made in United States
North Haven, CT
29 March 2023

34731161R00136